Anonymous

The Practical Speller Suitable for High and Public Schools

A Series of Graded Lessons

Anonymous

The Practical Speller Suitable for High and Public Schools
A Series of Graded Lessons

ISBN/EAN: 9783337779580

Printed in Europe, USA, Canada, Australia, Japan

Cover: Foto ©Thomas Meinert / pixelio.de

More available books at **www.hansebooks.com**

W. J. Gage & Co.'s Educational Series.

THE

PRACTICAL SPELLER

SUITABLE FOR HIGH AND PUBLIC SCHOOLS.

A SERIES OF GRADED LESSONS,

CONTAINING

THE WORDS IN GENERAL USE WITH ABBREVIATIONS, ETC; WORDS OF SIMILAR PRONUNCIATION AND DIFFERENT SPELLING; A COLLECTION OF THE MOST DIFFICULT WORDS IN THE LANGUAGE; WORDS COMMONLY MISSPELLED; A NUMBER OF LITERARY SELECTIONS WHICH MAY BE USED FOR DICTATION LESSONS, AND COMMITTED TO MEMORY BY THE PUPILS; AND THE LEADING GREEK AND LATIN ROOTS, PREFIXES AND AFFIXES.

Authorized for use in the Schools of Ontario.
Authorized for in the Schools of New Brunswick.
Authorized by the Council of Public Instruction, Quebec.
Authorized by the Council of Public Instruction, Manitoba.
Authorized by the Council of Public Instruction, British Columbia.

300TH THOUSAND.

W. J. GAGE & COMPANY, LIMITED

TORONTO.

PREFACE.

Is a Speller a Necessary School-Book? — The old-fashioned Spelling-Book has been discarded by teachers generally. Many valid objections were properly urged against its use, and it passed away.

Entire dependence upon *oral spelling* may also be fitly styled a method of bygone days. Unfortunately for the old spelling-book it was associated with all the folly and weakness of "oral spelling," and this partly accounts for its rejection.

What have the reformers given as a substitute for a Speller? They took our bread and have given in return but a stone. The bread even though a little stale was much more wholesome than the stone. In Canada parts of the lessons to be found in the Readers are taken as dictation lessons, and the pupils are turned loose on society to shock it by their bad spelling, and disgrace the schools which they attended, and in which they should have been taught. The Readers do not contain all the words that boys and girls will have to spell in life, and if they did, the lessons are not arranged in proper form for spelling lessons. Only a comparatively small portion of the Readers can be written from dictation in schools. Bad as were the old Spellers, they were infinitely better than nothing. This fact is now recognized in Great Britain and the United States, in both of which countries many valuable spelling-books have recently been issued. That these were necessary in England is clearly shown by the fact that at a recent Civil Service Examination "no less than 1,561 out of 1,972 failures were caused by spelling."

A practical dictation Speller is clearly a necessity, and this work has been prepared to supply an obvious want in the programme of Canadian schools. The claim to the name "Practical" is based on the fact that it is not a mere collection of thousands of "long-tailed words in *osity* and *ation*," but contains a graded series of lessons to teach the pupils the proper spelling of the words which all have to use.

Prominent Features. The book is divided into eight parts, as follows: —

PART I. contains the words in common use in daily life, together with abbreviations, forms, &c. These are the words that should first be learned. If a boy has to leave school early, he should at least know how to spell the words of every-day occurrence in connection with his business.

PART II. gives words liable to be spelled incorrectly because the same sounds are spelled in various ways in them.

PART III. contains words pronounced alike, but spelled differently with different meanings.

PART IV. contains a large collection of the most difficult words in common use, and is intended to supply material for a *general review*, or for spelling matches and tests.

PART V. Contains the words most commonly spelled incorrectly in Canadian schools. It was prepared from lists sent by many teachers. Pupils who can spell the words in Part V. will make few mistakes in spelling.

PART VI. contains spaces in which each pupil should write the words he is liable to misspell. This is a most important feature.

PART VII. contains selections for dictation lessons. They should be memorized by the pupils. They may thus aid in the training of language and character.

Part VIII. is devoted to etymology.

HINTS ON TEACHING SPELLING.

When should Pupils begin to Learn to Spell? — There should be no *oral* spelling, or *written* spelling either, *from memory*, during the first year and a half or two years of school life; yet pupils should be learning to spell from the start. How? By *copying*, COPYING, COPYING. By copying in script well-written sentences set by the teacher on the board. Sometimes these sentences may be taken from the primer, but they should generally be the language of the pupils themselves, including certain words given by the teacher.

Assigning Spelling Lessons. — The teacher should not merely say, "Prepare the tenth lesson," or, "Your dictation will be the first twelve lines on page 24." The pupils should pronounce after the teacher the words of the lesson, looking at them carefully as they do so. Peculiar or difficult words should be written on the blackboard, and spelled simultaneously by the pupils, and hints should be given to aid in the preparation of the lesson.

Preparing Spelling Lessons. — We wish to teach the forms of the words, not their sounds. Unfortunately, the forms of words do not always agree with the sounds in English; hence the form of a word must be impressed on the mind through the *eye*, and not the *ear*. It is perfectly clear therefore that the art of making good spellers consists in teaching pupils to see words accurately. The London Times once said, "Spelling is learnt by *reading*, and nothing but *reading* can teach *spelling*" It may be accepted as a rule that a good reader is always a good speller These facts all point the thoughtful teacher to the conclusion that we have already stated; — spelling depends on the power of *seeing with precision*. It follows that the exercise which compels the pupil to look most carefully at words must be the best method of preparing a spelling lesson. Unquestionably this exercise is *transcription*. Let the pupils copy on their slates the lesson to be prepared. The lesson may be copied as a home exercise, if due care be taken by the teacher in examining both spelling and writing. This is necessary in order to compel scrutinizing attention to the words to be copied The whole value of the exercise depends on this being done.

Repeating the letters of a word orally is of little lasting benefit. Make the pupils *see the words*, and if possible *never let a pupil see a word wrongly spelled.*

Testing Spelling Classes. — There are only two methods, *oral* and *written*. The *oral* method alone is of very little practical value. An American writer records the case of a young man "who won three prizes at spelling schools, but made five mistakes in spelling in a note written to a School Board." Oral spelling does not accustom the *eye* to the form of the word in writing. This is a fatal objection to it, and all modern teachers recommend that spelling lessons be conducted chiefly in writing

Correcting Spelling Lessons. - They must be corrected thoroughly. If proper preparation has been made as recommended *very few* errors will be made. In a large class the teacher will not be able to examine personally the book or slate of each pupil, except in the case of review lessons consisting of words previously misspelled in the class. These should always be examined by the teacher. In other lessons one of the following plans may be adopted: —

1. Pupils exchange slates, and the teacher gives the correct spelling word by word, the pupils marking those that are wrong.

2. Pupils retain their own slates, and different pupils are called on to spell the words. Those agreeing with the spelling given indicate by raising the hand, *before the teacher decides as to its correctness.* Marking as before.

3. Slates are exchanged and the corrections made as in No. 2.

4. While the teacher writes the correct spelling on the board, each pupil may correct his own work, and slates or books be exchanged for revision only. The latter method is probably the best with honest pupils.

In all cases where slates are exchanged the pupil owning the slate should have the right to appeal against the marking done by his neighbor.

Reviews. — Each pupil should write correctly the words which he misses, about five times, to impress the correct forms on his mind. In addition to this he ought to make a list at the end of his book of all the errors he makes. From this list the teacher should prepare his reviews. The words missed are the only words that need to be taught. "Learn [illegible] in the first." *Review regularly.*

General Suggestions. — 1. The teacher should always articulate clearly and pronounce correctly when giving words for spelling.

2. Never overstress the pronunciation of a word in order to indicate its spelling.

3. Allow only one trial in spelling orally or in writing.

4. In spelling orally, the divisions into syllables should be marked by slight pauses but in no other way.

5. Do not assign lessons too difficult for the pupils who have to prepare them. This compels the pupils to spell badly.

6. It is desirable that spelling should be taught to a considerable extent by means of *compositions*, in order to give the pupils practice in spelling the words in their own vocabularies.

7. In some of the dictation lessons in this book time may be saved by having only the words in *italics* spelled. The teacher should read the whole sentence and emphasize the words to be spelled.

PREFACE TO NEW AND ENLARGED EDITION.

With a view to perfecting the Practical Speller, and making it in every respect worthy of the name "practical," two new chapters have been added, Parts V. and VI.

Part V. was compiled from lists of the words commonly misspelled in schools in all parts of the Dominion, and it will therefore be a most important addition to the book. It is a fact worthy of note that the pupils throughout Canada fail in the spelling of nearly the same words.

Part VI. is intended to be the special spelling book of the individual child who owns the book. It will form the best basis for reviewing, not only during school life, but in after years.

PART I.

FAMILIAR WORDS.

The lists in Part I. contain the words in common use in every-day life. They are the words which every person who writes at all must use, and which every child should therefore learn to spell.

They may be used for oral spelling or dictation lessons for the class or exercise book. The latter method is much to be preferred.

The difficult words are repeated so as to give a review lesson about once a week.

Dictation lessons in sentence form are given at intervals. They may serve as models for teachers, who may, if they wish, include the words of each lesson in sentences. It will be a good plan for advanced pupils to write sentences of their own, including the words dictated by the teacher.

The words are arranged in three columns, and the simplest are placed in the first column and the most difficult in the last. Each lesson may thus be assigned to three different classes. Pupils in the Second Book, for instance, might have to spell only the words of the first column, those in the Third Book the words in the first and second columns, and those in the Fourth Book the whole lesson. The Third and Fourth Book classes would in this way be reviewing the work of previous sessions. Many of the lessons are so simple that each lesson may be assigned as a whole to even Second Book students.

1. *At Home.*

house	par lor	gar ret
door	clos et	at tic
room	pan try	cel lar
porch	kitch en	cham ber
floor	win dow	bed room
hall	cup board	li bra ry
en try	thresh old	ve ran da
stair case	din ing-room	bal co ny
ward robe	bath-room	pi az za

2. *In the Parlor.*

vase	lounge	pic ture
chair	so fa	por trait
grate	car pet	brack et
screen	cur tain	cush ion
frame	tas sel	pi a no
ta ble	mir ror	ot to man

3. *In the Dining-Room.*

cup	plate	cru et
spoon	sau cer	cast er
bowl	la dle	tu reen
glass	nap kin	plat ter
knife	sil ver	tum bler
fork	pitch er	side board
tray	ta ble	tea-urn

4. *In the Kitchen.*

stove	ba sin	ov en
range	tow el	bas ket
tongs	grat er	kin dlings
brush	skil let	dust-pan
broom	ket tle	flat i ron
pail	grid dle	and i ron
soap	sauce pan	grid i ron

5. *In the Pantry.*

pan	chest	dip per
jar	flask	strain er
jug	fruit	skim mer
pail	can is ter	pic kles
tray	crock er y	vict uals
sieve	tin-ware	pre serves

6. *Chamber and Garret.*

beds	tow el	mat tress
trunk	bol ster	wash-stand
lamp	blan ket	ba sin
quilt	cra dle	cov er let
sheets	bed stead	coun ter pane

7. *Review of Difficult Words.*

knife	**vase**	**fruit**
tas sel	**cru et**	**sieve**
la dle	**tu reen**	**sau cer**
por trait	**pre serves**	**ba sin**
can is ter	**bal co ny**	**vict uals**
pi az za	**li bra ry**	**cup board**

8. Kindness, neatness, order, piety, and a cheerful heart make home the happy place it is so often found to be. There is joy as real by the cottage fireside, as in the most splendid abodes of wealth and luxury.

9. *In the Shed and Tool-house.*

saw	pole	yoke
file	spade	chain
nail	sledge	shov el
spike	wedge	trow el
hoe	le ver	meas ure
rake	bee tle	crow bar
pick	cleav er	grind stone

10. *In the Barn and Yard.*

pump	crib	cra dle
trough	hay	reap er
spout	rake	roll er
flail	straw	har row
sleigh	grain	cut ter
scythe	fod der	har ness

sic kle	mow er	gran a ry
wag on	bug gy	pitch fork
sad dle	hal ter	cul ti vator

11. *Family and Relatives.*

son	fa ther	daugh ter
wife	moth er	grand child
aunt	cous in	grand son
niece	broth er	grand daugh ter
pa pa	breth ren	grand mother
un cle	hus band	grand fath er
sis ter	mam ma	half-sis ter
par ent	neph ew	half-broth er

12. *Household Names.*

kin	friend	youth
lad	babe	val et
boy	maid	in fant
man	dame	la dy
men	cook	ba by
girl	child	ma tron
lass	nurse	maid en
wait er	but ler	vis i tor
wait ress	stew ard	rel a tive
mis tress	coach man	do mes tic
ser vant	chil dren	bach e lor
wo man	house wife	gen tle man
wo men	house maid	gov er ness
fam i ly	house hold	house keep er

13.

"We are all here!
Father, mother, sister, brother,
All who hold each other dear.
Each chair is filled — we 're all at home;
To-night let no cold stranger come:
Let gentle Peace assert her power,
And kind Affection rule the hour."

14. *Review of Difficult Words.*

sledge	**shov el**	**gran a ry**
flail	**meas ure**	**wo men**
niece	**bee tle**	**daugh ter**
scythe	**cous in**	**bach e lor**
trough	**un cle**	**gov er ness**
sleigh	**neph ew**	**vis i tor**
friend	**val et**	**rel a tive**

15.

Sister and I love mamma. A babe is an infant, or young child. I may say IT and ITS of a baby, though a boy or girl; as, IT is like ITS papa. Our uncle and aunt are husband and wife. Their children are our cousins. A nephew is a son, and a niece a daughter, of one's brother or sister. In our household are parents, children, and servants. Father is master. Mother is matron, housewife, or mistress of the family. The domestics are men, women, youths, and maidens. They are steward, butler, valet, coachman, and waiter; housekeeper, governess, nurse, cook, waitress, housemaid, etc Our relatives near of kin are grandfather, grandmother, etc.

16. *Animal Food.*

ham
veal
pork
beef
loin
fish
chop
egg
bird
fowl
meat
curd

milk
lamb
game
steak
tripe
flesh
cream
cheese
but ter
oys ter
liv er
ba con

hon ey
cut let
rash er
chick en
mut ton
sir loin
cus tard
sau sage
beef steak
sar dine
sal mon
had dock

17. *Vegetable Food. (Unprepared.)*

rice
corn
peas
fruit
pear
plum
maize
wheat
beans
peach
squash

rye
oats
cress
prune
grape
tur nip
cel e ry
bar ley
let tuce
car rot
cab bage

pars nip
on ion
pump kin
mel on
rad ish
rhu barb
spin ach
po ta to
to ma to
cu cum ber
as par a gus

18. *Vegetable Food. (Prepared.)*

bun	dough	pan cake
roll	muf fin	crack er
meal	krul ler	dough nut
flour	bis cuit	dump ling
bread	waf fle	blanc mange
mush	catch up	pud ding
soup	but ter	sand wich
tea	gru el	co coa
broth	pas try	cof fee
sauce	jel ly	choc o late
pie	por ridge	lem on ade
stew	gra vy	vin e gar

19. *Review of Difficult Words.*

steak	**oys ter**	**rhu barb**
maize	**hon ey**	**spin ach**
rye	**sir loin**	**blanc mange**
flour	**sal mon**	**sand wich**
sauce	**sau sage**	**cel e ry**
stew	**sar dine**	**choc o late**
dough	**on ion**	**as par a gus**

20. Bread is made of the flour or meal of grain. Pastry is pies, tarts, cake, and the like, made in part of paste, or dough. Animal food is a part of our victuals, viands, diet, or fare. Food is flesh, fish, vegetables, and all things eaten for nutriment, or nourishment. Use water, milk, tea, coffee, cocoa, chocolate, or lemonade, for a beverage, or drink [illegible] or wild [illegible] for food. I like a mutton-chop, a leg of lamb, a loin of veal, a sirloin beefsteak, pork ham, a rasher of bacon, sausage, tripe, or liver. We eat curd, cheese, cream, butter, etc. In our garden we have corn, peas, beans, onions, lettuce, carrots, squashes, celery, parsley, tomatoes, fruit. In our fields we raise wheat, maize, barley, oats, buckwheat, potatoes, turnips, carrots, etc.

21. *Setting the Table.*

(The teacher may use the names of his own pupils.)

Bertha, you may spread the cloth upon the table; Laura, bring the knives and forks; Caroline, the cups and saucers; Lucile, carry the plates; Helen, the spoons; Louise, go to the drawer for the clean napkins; as soon as the water boils in the tea-kettle, Frank can pour it on the tea and coffee; Albert, go to the cellar for the cream, — do not spill it on the stairs; Minnie, bring the sugar; Harold, go quickly for the covered dishes for the oat-meal and potatoes; as soon as Charles has taken the roast-beef from the oven, you can thicken the gravy; William, place the chairs around the table; how neatly you have arranged the red and white celery, Edward!

22. *Clothing for the Head and Neck.*

scarf	mask	cha peau
hat	tip pet	hel met
cap	cra vat	neck tie
wig	col lar	neck lace
veil	bon net	muf fler
hood	tur ban	neck cloth

23. *Clothing for the Body.*

skirt	robe	cor set
belt	cape	a pron
cloak	gown	man tle
frock	sash	sur tout
shawl	shirt	spen cer
blouse	flounce	sur plice
basque	tu nic	pe lisse
kilt	gir dle	che mise
vest	dust er	wrap per
coat	bod ice	waist coat

24. *Clothing for the Limbs.*

gloves	clogs	draw ers
tights	muffs	stock ings
sleeves	gai ters	trou sers
smalls	san dals	breech es
boots	mit tens	wrist bands
shoes	slip pers	over alls
hose	leg gins	moc ca sons
socks	gaunt lets	pan ta loons

25. *Material for Clothing.*

thread	felt	edg ing
frill	lace	lin sey
gauze	pop lin	can vas

plaid	wool	tick ing
print	cot ton	wors ted
plush	mus lin	cam bric
baize	bea ver	broad clot
tape	dam ask	al pac a
jean	wool len	cal i co
yarn	bat ting	sat i net

26. *Material for Clothing.*

braid	gimp	mo reen
crape	hook	nan keen
cloth	fringe	bro cade
twill	rub ber	mo roc co
tweed	lin en	cash mere
chintz	sat in	leath er
serge	vel vet	kip skin
lawn	tar tan	cow hide
silk	tas sel	calf skin
flax	ging ham	trim mings

27. *Review of Difficult Words.*

shawl	bod ice	ging ham
basque	sur tout	can vas
veil	pe lisse	calf skins
tights	che mise	cal i co
plaid	wrap per	al pac a
baize	cha peau	mo roc co
serge	trou sers	cash mere

28. *Dress.*

Dress has a moral effect upon the conduct of mankind. Let any gentleman find himself with dirty boots, old surtout, soiled neckcloth, and a general negligence of dress, he will, in all probability, find a corresponding disposition by negligence of *address*. – *Sir John Barrington.*

We sacrifice to Dress, till household joys
And comforts cease. Dress drains our cellar dry,
And keeps our larder lean; puts out our fires,
And introduces Hunger, Frost, and Woe,
Where Peace and Hospitality might reign – *Cowper.*

29. *Parts of the Head and Neck.*

lip	brow	pu pil
eye	tooth	eye lid
ear	brain	eye ball
jaw	scalp	eye lash
gum	beard	eye brow
chin	cheek	tem ple
nose	skull	nos tril
face	mouth	whis kers
hair	voice	fore head
head	tongue	mus tache
neck	throat	wind pipe

30. *Parts of the Trunk and Waist.*

rib	heart	bo som
hip	chest	ten don
skin	breast	bow els

bone	nerve	kid ney
pore	spine	mus cle
back	lungs	stom ach
vein	trunk	en trails
loin	groin	shoul der
side	blood	back bone
flesh	bod y	breast bone
waist	liv er	ar te ry
flank	sin ew	ab do men

31. *Parts of the Limbs.*

leg	limb	el bow
toe	hand	an kle
arm	palm	in step
feet	knee	fin ger
nail	joint	arm pit
foot	pulse	fore arm
heel	thigh	knuc kle
sole	wrist	knee pan
calf	thumb	knee joint

32. *The Fairy's Gift.*

A lazy girl, who liked to live in comfort and do nothing, asked her fairy godmother to give her a good genius to do everything for her. On the instant the fairy called ten dwarfs, who dressed and washed the little girl, and combed her hair and fed her, and so on. All was done so nicely that she was happy except for the thought that they would go away. "To prevent that," said the godmother, "I will place them permanently in your ten pretty little fingers." And they are there yet.

33. *Words Relating to Appetite.*

hun ger	ea ger	crav ing
thirst	greed y	long ing
gorge	dain ty	rav en ous
quench	health y	vo ra cious
de sire	re gale	pam pered
de vour	sat is fy	glut ton ous

34. *Articles of Convenience.*

cane	va lise	par a sol
whip	satch el	spec ta cles
purse	lan tern	um brel la
strap	eye glass	o ver shoes
comb	card-case	wa ter-proof
brush	dust er	hand ker chief
brooch	buc kle	lead pen cil

35. *Vehicles.*

gig	coach	ba rouche
hack	chaise	bar row
cart	cou pé	char i ot
cab	bug gy	pha e ton
dray	cut ter	om ni bus
sled	wag gon	dil i gence
sleigh	car riage	horse-car

36. *Review of Difficult Words.*

skull	brooch	va lise
nerve	sleigh	buc kle
calf	chaise	ba rouche
palm	tongue	pha e ton
thigh	mus tache	par a sol
wrist	stom ach	spec ta cles
thumb	knuc kle	o ver shoes

37. *Schools.*

high	dis trict	in dus tri al
pub lic	col lege	di vin i ty
mod el	gram mar	a cad e my
grad ed	board ing	sem i na ry
un ion	pri ma ry	com mer cial
nor mal	med i cal	u ni ver si ty
pri vate	clas si cal	kin der gar ten

38. *On the Way to School.*

slow	road	gate way
dust	lane	rail ing
mud	street	av e nue
hail	track	pave ment
snow	park	guide-post
rain	al ley	lamp-post
frost	gut ter	side walk
smoke	cross ing	curb stone

39. *In the School-room.*

desk	pa per	satch el
bell	fer ule	pen cil
map	rat tan	cray on
chart	black board	mon i tor
clock	chil dren	as sist ant
book	teach er	reg is ter
slate	point er	ink-bot tle
globe	stu dent	dic tion a ry
chalk	rub ber	ap pa ra tus

40. *What Pupils do.*

read	at tend	con strue
write	stud y	trans late
parse	re cite	ex am ine
solve	de claim	rec ol lect
think	reck on	re mem ber
learn	com pose	cal cu late
lis ten	com pute	an a lyze

41.

Man's *life* involves birth, breath, warmth, care, growth, strength, youth, love, mercy, attention, direction, the finite, death, etc. With mind we connect brain, thought, sense, school, study, perception, reflection, application, memory, consideration, investigation, wisdom, etc. Schools are known as public, common, graded, high, union, select, model, normal, parish, commercial, preparatory, primary, reformatory, agricultural, scientific, medical, divinity, kindergarten, etc. Do you attend an academy, a seminary, a college, or a university? Connected with schools are the trustees, the instructor or teacher, the professor, principal, assistant, monitor, monitress, etc. Belonging to schools are text-books, apparatus, paper, colors, a lexicon or dictionary, a clock, chart, pencil, crayon, magnet, blackboard, library, gazetteer, cyclopædia, pens, etc. At intermission and after dismission there are many games; as, base-ball, leap-frog, quoits, croquet, lacrosse, cricket, etc.

42. *What a Boy or Girl should be.*

kind	hon est	stu di ous
good	truth ful	rev er ent
frank	ear nest	gen er ous
brave	hope ful	en er get ic
no ble	help ful	cour a geous
po lite	care ful	o be di ent
hap py	joy ous	in dus tri ous
lov ing	thought ful	af fec tion ate

43. *What a Boy or Girl should not be.*

bad	cru el	wick ed
mean	self ish	heed less
proud	un kind	im po lite
la zy	fret ful	de ceit ful
sulk y	pro fane	dis hon est
sau cy	im pure	cow ard ly
stin gy	vi cious	quar rel some

44. *Boys sometimes are —*

dull	nois y	stead fast
wise	mer ry	un ti dy
cross	stu pid	un civ il
rude	pa tient	re spect ful
man ly	sin cere	im per ti nent
bus y	faith ful	bois ter ous
wit ty	play ful	in ge ni ous
jol ly	mirth ful	in gen u ous

45. *Girls sometimes are —*

shy	kind ly	tri fling
bold	gen tle	tat tling
weak	si lent	bash ful
sil ly	fee ble	sim per ing
gid dy	clum sy	im pul sive
so ber	haugh ty	a gree a ble
se date	anx ious	friv o lous
live ly	aim less	non sen si cal

46. *Review of Difficult Words.*

high	pen cil	haugh ty
dew	cray on	anx ious
chalk	re cite	mon i tor
parse	hon est	friv o lous
solve	vi cious	in ge ni ous
un ion	bus y	o be di ent
gram mar	pa tient	ap pa ra tus
satch el	sin cere	dic tion a ry

67. *Words used in Tables.*

inch	gill	sec ond
foot	pint	min ute
yard	quart	de gree
rod	peck	gal lon
mile	grain	bush el
mill	dram	scru ple
cent	ounce	far thing
ton	pound	guin ea
tun	a cre	dol lar
pence	quar ter	fur long

68. *Seasons, Months, and Days.*

Spring	May	Sun day
Sum mer	June	Sab bath
Au tumn	Ju ly	Mon day
Win ter	Au gust	Tues day
Jan u a ry	Sep tem ber	Wed nes day
Feb ru a ry	Oc to ber	Thurs day
March	No vem ber	Fri day
A pril	De cem ber	Sat ur day

69. *The Days of the Months.*

Thirty days hath September,
April, June, and November,
February twenty eight alone;
All the rest have thirty-one,
Except in leap-year: at this time
February's days are twenty-nine

50. *Weights and Measures.*

dry
troy
square
cu bic
ster ling
for eign
li quid
Eng lish
mis cel la ne ous
apoth e ca ries'
av oir du pois
long measure

51. *Words used in Arithmetic.*

sign
u nit
di git
num ber
fac tor
ci pher
fig ure
quo tient
frac tion
ze ro
ra tio
ex change
a mount
pro duct
de ci mal
in ter est
quan ti ty
min u end
di vi sor
div i dend
re main der
ro ta tion
dis count
ad di tion
di vis ion
sub trac tion
sub tra hend
part ner ship
in sur ance
per cent age
nu mer a tor
de nom i na tor
mul ti pli cand

52. *Punctuation.*

dash
brace
co lon
com ma
ca ret
ac cent
brack et
hy phen
pe ri od
el lip sis
as ter isk
sem i co lon
pa ren the sis
ex cla ma tion
in ter ro ga tion

53. *Things Written or Printed.*

verse	po e try	es say
prose	stan za	re port
hymn	coup let	re view
speech	son net	jour nal
rhyme	bal lad	ad dress
psalm	no tice	o ra tion
po em	post er	cer tif i cate
i tem	pla card	par a graph

54. *Writing Materials.*

quire	ream	blot ter
pen	pa per	pen knife
quill	let ter	di a ry
pen cil	tab let	e ras er
wa fer	fools cap	mu ci lage
rul er	rub ber	en ve lope
cray on	ink stand	port fo lio

55. *Review of Difficult Words.*

inch	**scru ple**	**jour nal**
quart	**guin ea**	**pen knife**
ounce	**Au gust**	**Wed nes day**
sign	**Tues day**	**sub trac tion**
verse	**quo tient**	**el lip sis**
hymn	**ci pher**	**mu ci lage**
rhyme	**hy phen**	**par a graph**
psalm	**coup let**	**sem i co lon**

56. *Domestic Animals.*

cat	calf	goat
kid	calves	mas tiff
mule	ox en	stock
colt	span iel	swine
don key	horse	herd
hound	sheep	beast
lamb	flock	cat tle
cow	heif er	ter ri er

57. *Wild Animals.*

deer	cam el	ze bra
wolf	bea ver	mon key
bear	er mine	squir rel
lynx	mar ten	wood chuck
mink	wea sel	rein deer
moose	rac coon	an te lope
lion	jack al	por cu pine
ti ger	leop ard	buf fa lo
pan ther	hy e na	el e phant

58. *Birds.*

owl	spar row	con dor
crow	lin net	blue jay
wren	cuck oo	blue bird
gull	par rot	bob o link
stork	mar tin	gold finch

hawk	swal low	chick a dee
thrush	ca na ry	wood peck er
ea gle	o ri ole	whip poor will

59. *Don't kill the Birds.*

Don't kill the birds, the pretty birds,
That sing about your door,
Soon as the joyous spring has come,
And chilling storms are o'er.

60. *Reptiles and Insects.*

ant	midge	tor toise
wasp	hor net	cock roach
gnat	gad-fly	ka ty did
moth	bee tle	mos qui to
toad	spi der	but ter fly
frog	crick et	bum ble bee
newt	liz ard	grass hop per
snake	tad pole	cat er pil lar
worm	ser pent	drag on fly

61. *Climate.*

hot	sun ny	pleas ant
dry	fog gy	ge ni al
cold	mist y	trop i cal
cool	balm y	health ful
mild	cloud y	de light ful
moist	sul try	sa lu bri ous
warm	storm y	tem pest u ous

62. *Games and Amusements.*

sled	quoits	bil liards
kite	chess	base-ball
hoop	wick et	curl ing
ball	cro quet	ten nis
bow	crick et	foot-ball
tag	check ers	fish-hook
skates	draughts	la crosse

63. *In a Mechanic's Shop.*

awl	bit	bev el
bench	vise	au ger
plane	lathe	gim let
square	forge	pin cers
punch	an vil	nip pers
shears	ham mer	pul ley
wrench	mal let	com pass
gauge	chis el	whet stone

64. *Review of Difficult Words.*

lamb	**vise**	**chis el**
calves	**heif er**	**el e phant**
lynx	**liz ard**	**squir rel**
wren	**tor toise**	**mos qui to**
hawk	**balm y**	**o ri ole**
gnat	**draughts**	**por cu pine**
quoits	**ieop ard**	**ca na ry**
awl	**rein deer**	**tem pest u ous**
wrench	**au ger**	**sa lu bri ous**

65. *In a Country Store.*

hops	tal low	cut ler y
salt	can dles	gro cer ies
shoes	wick ing	dry-goods
shot	match es	grass-seed
glue	black ing	clothes-pins
tar	pol ish	va nil la
cloth	feath ers	i sin glass
yarn	var nish	gun pow der
starch	flax seed	con fec tion er y

66. *Parts of a Carriage and Harness.*

hub	rein	col lar
tire	strap	head stall
spoke	girth	blink ers
fel loe	trace	check-rein
wheel	hames	crup per
bolt	bri dle	breech ing
screw	hal ter	breast plate
ax le	snaf fle	linch pin
dash er	buc kle	sur cin gle

67. *Parts of a Watch or Clock.*

case	spring	jew el
face	le ver	hair spring
hand	piv ot	pen du lum
wheel	riv et	reg u la tor
cog	weight	bal ance-wheel

Lost yesterday, somewhere between sunrise and sunset, two golden hours, each set with sixty diamond minutes. No reward is offered, for they are gone forever.

68. *Words Relating to Travel.*

rove	tour	cruis ing
roam	tramp	wan der
stroll	ram ble	trav erse
cruise	saun ter	mi grate
jaunt	jour ney	ex cur sion
trudge	voy age	ex pe di tion
train	sail ing	prom e nade

69. *Post-Office and Railway Station.*

mail	bag gage	brake man
train	lug gage	con duc tor
freight	pack age	tel e graph
tick et	ex press	tel e gram
de pot	en gine	news pa per
let ter	pam phlet	val en tine
par cel	mag a zine	post mas ter
bun dle	doc u ment	lo co mo tive

70. *Common Trees.*

oak	birch	al der
fir	spruce	pop lar
ash	ce dar	lin den

elm	hol ly	wil low
pine	ha zel	hem lock
beech	ma ple	lo cust
larch	chest nut	hick o ry

71. *Review of Difficult Words.*

shoes	piv ot	jour ney
rein	riv et	pop lar
fel loe	de pot	en gine
screw	pam phlet	sur cin gle
weight	ma ple	mag a zine
cruise	chest nut	tel e graph
tour	feath ers	prom e nade
freight	rein deer	i sin glass

72. *Review.*

PROVISIONS are eatables, or food, collected and stored. The miller takes toll from the farmer, for grinding the grist. He sells flour, meal, bran, shorts, feed, etc. The baker makes bread, biscuit, tarts, cake, and other pastry; the chandler, candles. A grocer is a trader who deals in tea, coffee, chocolate, and cocoa; sugar, molasses, syrup, and honey; preserved meat and fish, as dried beef, tongue, pork, bacon, ham, shad, codfish, herring, salmon, mackerel, anchovies, and isinglass; spices, comfits, preserves, pickles, candies, nuts, ginger, pepper, nutmeg, cassia, cloves, mustard, allspice, cinnamon, almonds, raisins, gelatine, extracts, and marmalade; granular food, as hominy, oat-meal, tapioca, arrow-root, and corn-starch; and illuminators, as matches, candles, lard oil, sperm oil, coal oil, etc.

73. *Things we can Do.*

see
hear
touch
smell
taste
eat
sew
walk
talk
feel
love
pray

think
yawn
play
dance
sleep
work
sweep
scrub
draw
swim
skate
slide

smile
laugh
groan
moan
cough
sneeze
breathe
waltz
gos sip
scrib ble
whis per
whis tle

74. *Various Classes of People.*

serf
nun
monk
saint
priest
guide
quack
vas sal
var let
dea con

pas tor
a gent
fac tor
stew ard
driv er
run ner
sex ton
sa vant
gym nast
work man

states man
sen a tor
cit i zen
of fi cer
la bor er
ap pren tice
op er a tor
op er a tive
fin an cier
pol i ti cian

75. *Trades.*

tai lor
weav er

print er
join er

gold smith
per fum er

hat ter
sad dler
coop er
turn er

ma son
black smith
car pen ter
bind er

mil li ner
dress mak er
ma chin ist
plumb er

76. *Occupations.*

nurse
clerk
farm er
sai lor
pur ser
por ter
hos tler
mil ler

bar ber
butch er
min er
bank er
cash ier
drug gist
mer chant
sales man

carv er
seam stress
re port er
jan i tor
gar den er
ca ter er
sta tion er
pho tog ra pher

77. *Professions.*

po et
ac tor
au thor
law yer
doc tor
sur geon

teach er
art ist
paint er
ed i tor
sculp tor
en grav er

or a tor
mu si cian
en gi neer
sur vey or
phy si cian
his to ri an

78. *Public Officers.*

judge
bai liff
jus tice

war den
turn key
con sta ble

au di tor
ma gis trate
al der man

sher iff	trus tee	com mis sion er
may or	po lice man	su per in tend ent
as ses sor	col lec tor	in spec tor

79. *Review.*

EXCHANGE is the mode of settling accounts or debts between persons living at a distance from each other, by exchanging orders or drafts, called *bills of exchange*. *Foreign bills* are drawn in one country and payable in another. *Inland bills* are drawn and made payable in the same country Trade is the exchange, or buying or selling, of goods. It is known as *domestic*, *inland*, or *home*; *foreign*, *wholesale*, *retail*, etc. Each man has his business, vocation, office, pursuit, or calling; as a banker, president, director, secretary, cashier, teller, book-keeper, treasurer, broker, buyer, factor, agent, dealer, trader, jobber, peddler, huckster, vendor, merchant, salesman, shopman, tradesman, financier, auctioneer, etc. Finance is the income of a state or ruler, or the public funds. Specie, hard money, or coin is copper, silver, or gold, stamped at public mints, and used in commerce. It is known as cents, dollars, pence, shillings, pounds, guineas, guilders, ducats, etc. Bullion is uncoined gold or silver, in bars, ingots or in the mass.

80. *State Officers.*

chief	sul tan	au to crat
king	bar on	dic ta tor
queen	prin cess	gov er nor
duke	duch ess	sov er eign
prince	mon arch	pres i dent

pope	pre mier	gen er al
prel ate	em press	ad mi ral
bish op	em per or	rep re sent a tive

81. *Review of Difficult Words.*

touch	whis tle	pre mier
walk	bai liff	cit i zen
talk	gym nast	fin an cier
monk	plumb er	ma chin ist
guide	hos tler	sta tion er
clerk	cash ier	phy si cian
laugh	sher iff	sur vey or
cough	bar on	sov er eign
waltz	mon arch	pho tog ra pher

82. *Water Channels.*

pipe	ditch	ca nal
drain	trench	cul vert
spout	moat	si phon
duct	sluice	con duit
race	gut ter	a que duct
dike	sew er	wa ter-course

83. *Colors.*

red	pink	brown
blue	drab	am ber
green	scar let	mad der
yel low	crim son	pur ple
or ange	car mine	ma roon
li lac	ver mil ion	vi o let
in di go	lav en der	sal mon

84. *The Farm.*

sod	pool	swale
vale	wood	lane
hill	house	fence
dell	ridge	wall
dale	creek	path
bush	hedge	road
rock	copse	barn
bank	yard	drain

85. *Soil, Implements, &c.*

soil	a cres	mow er
clay	gar den	dai ry
loam	fer tile	or chard
spade	ster ile	mead ow
sand	cra dle	sic kle
churn	har row	wood land
ground	bar ren	plas ter
earth	up land	barn yard
chain	pas ture	ar a ble
flail	low land	al lu vi al
fork	reap er	ag ri cul ture
hoe	gyp sum	cul ti va tor

86. *Products of the Farm.*

rye	cow	clo ver
oats	bull	fod der
hay	husks	bar ley

sow	feed	red top
pig	calf	stub ble
hog	peas	mel ons
ham	seed	ap ples
lard	pear	cit rons
pork	milk	car rots

87. *Products of the Farm.*

chaff	hides	gar lic
straw	pelt	tur nip
sheaf	hens	rhu barb
stock	eggs	pump kin
crops	curd	spin ach
ewe	whey	buck wheat
ram	corn	po ta to
lamb	beets	to ma to
veal	hops	musk mel on
beef		

88. *Products of the Farm.*

hemp	sheep	tal low
grapes	steer	bul lock
plums	swine	tur keys
fruit	cheese	rad ish
grain	cream	ma nure
peach	ba con	bil ber ry
beans	sau sage	cran ber ry
maize	poul try	goose ber ry
wool	but ter	black ber ry

89. *Products of the Farm.*

wheat	thyme	a pri cot
grass	fleece	cu cum ber
goose	quince	beech nuts
geese	pars nip	but ter nuts
herbs	pars ley	ox en
herds	let tuce	cher ries
squash	cur rants	rasp ber ries
ducks	clo ver	straw ber ries
drake	cel er y	huc kle ber ries
chicks	tim o thy	as par a gus

90. *Review.*

HUSBANDRY, or farming, is the cultivation, or tillage, of the ground. Horticulture is the art of cultivating gardens Agriculture is the art of cultivating the soil, generally in fields of many acres. It includes chopping, yoking, driving, logging, stabling, clearing, fencing, ploughing, sowing, dragging, rolling, marking, planting, hoeing, spading, weeding, digging, picking, mowing, cradling, harvesting, housing, and threshing, — all the work of raising crops. Lands worked by tenants are too often sterile, barren, or worn out. A large farm may have arable or tillable upland, fertile, rocky, sandy, or loamy; pastures and meadows; hills, caves, dales, dells, glades, roads, paths, woods, forests, springs, ponds, streams, brooks, creeks, coves, lowlands, chasms, swales, swamps, bogs, pools, sloughs, etc. The husbandman, or farmer, needs a good farmhouse, barn, stable, shed, and other buildings; marl, lime, gypsum, guano, compost, barn-yard manure, muck, phosphate, bone-dust, and other fertilizers; and a plough, colter, harrow, cultivator, axe, hoe, spade, shovel, rake, roller, sickle, cradle, reaper, mower, pitchfork, etc. Productive farms yield corn, wheat, rye, oats, barley, buckwheat, peas, beans, millet, and other bread-stuffs; clover, red-top, timothy, blue-grass, and other grasses; potatoes, onions, beets, carrots, turnips, tomatoes, rhubarb, asparagus, parsnips, parsley, celery, lettuce, tobacco, flax, hemp, cotton, wool, fruits, flowers, berries, melons, meat, poultry, game, etc.

91. *Books and Papers.*

book	vol ume	re port ing
news	lo cal	mag a zine
tales	jour nal	com mer cial
births	col umn	sub scrib er
deaths	morn ing	jour nal ist
i tem	e ven ing	ed i tor
dai ly	ar ti cle	ad ver tis er
week ly	re port er	con trib u tor
for eign	tel e gram	mem o ran da

92. *Stationery.*

note	pen cil	rul ers
pens	wa fers	rub ber
ream	blot ter	pen rack
sheet	eye lets	port fo lios
quire	fold ers	e ras er
quills	bind ers	di a ries
cards	brush es	al ma nac
chess	cray ons	dom i noes

slates	let ter	mu ci lage
sponge	pa per	en ve lopes
parch ment	pam phlet	pen hold er
blank book	pen knives	cat a logue

93. *Metals and Minerals.*

tin	i ron	co balt
lead	quartz	ag ate
gold	mi ca	gyp sum
brass	cop per	gran ite
steel	sil ver	mer cu ry
zinc	nick el	plum ba go

94. *Diseases.*

cold	ca tarrh	scrof u la
croup	mea sles	pleu ri sy
mumps	head ache	neu ral gi a
gout	chil blains	pneu mo ni a
spasms	tooth ache	pa ral y sis
fe ver	hic cough	rheu ma tism
a gue	nau se a	con sump tion
col ic	chol er a	whoop ing cough
bron chi tis	epi lep sy	di ar rhœ a

95. *Nationalities.*

Dutch	Prus sian	I tal ian
French	Pol ish	A si at ic
I rish	In di an	Amer i can

Eng lish	Hin doo	A ra bi an
Turk ish	Chi nese	Si am ese
Span ish	He brew	Es qui maux
Rus sian	Af ri can	Nor we gi an
Ger man	Aus tri an	Eu ro pe an

96. *Review.*

MEDICINE relates to the prevention or cure of diseases of the body. An ailment is a morbid state of the body, not an acute disease. The patient had an infectious and malignant disease. Did he prefer allopathy, hydropathy, homœopathy, or botanic practice? A complaint is a slight disorder. A malady is a chronic or painful disorder. Was the fever scarlet, yellow, typhus, gastric, bilious, or typhoid? The delirious invalid, a glutton and a cripple, suffered with the gout Man suffers from diarrhœa, toothache, rheumatism, cholera, dyspepsia, diphtheria, pneumonia, chilblains, dysentery, insanity, epilepsy, erysipelas, neuralgia, constipation, hydrophobia, congestion, inflammation, bronchitis, carbuncles, consumption, paralysis, nausea, pleurisy, etc.

97. *Religions and Sects.*

Pa gan	Jew ish	U ni ta ri an
Mor mon	Bap tist	Spir it u al ist
Buddh ist	Meth o dist	Swe den bor gi an
Brah min	Cal vin ist	Pres by te ri an
Chris tian	Or tho dox	E pis co pa li an
Lu ther an	Cath o lic	Con gre ga tion al
Qua ker	Prot es tant	Mo ham me dan

98. *Church Officers.*

priest	pas tor	bish op
clerk	preach er	cu rate
dean	vic ar	e van ge list
par son	rab bi	mis sion a ry
trus tee	el der	col por teur
chap lain	dea con	cler gy man

99. *Names of God.*

God	Je sus	Me di a tor
Son	Fa ther	A noint ed
Lord	Mak er	Cre a tor
Lamb	Sav iour	Je ho vah
Word	Spir it	Al might y
Judge	Ho ly Ghost	Re deem er
Christ	Pre serv er	In ter ces sor

100. *Review.*

JUDAISM is the religious doctrines and rites of the Hebrews, or Jews; also, conformity to the Jewish rites and ceremonies. The ending *ism* means doctrine, sect, or party; as, Romanism, Protestantism, Mohammedanism, paganism, pantheism, fanaticism, polytheism, monotheism, materialism, formalism, mysticism, scepticism, etc. Denominations of Christians are known as Catholic, Episcopal, Lutheran, Calvinist, Methodist, Reformed, Moravian, Unitarian, Trinitarian, Presbyterian, Congregational, Quaker or Friend, Baptist, etc. We should not be low, mean, base, vile, proud, sinful, wicked, haughty, vicious, profane, sceptical, profligate, irreverent, impious, — a scoffer, scorner, mocker, bigot, or an unbeliever. We should be meek, humble, reverent, faithful, moral, virtuous, pious, pure, devout, righteous, and godly. Strive for humility, purity, piety, spirituality, sanctity, and holiness. Avoid hypocrisy, profanity, irreverence, idolatry, and ungodliness.

101. *Review.*

Many devout people sing hymns and psalms, chant, kneel, pray, fast, give alms, praise God, implore, beseech, adore, invoke, worship, etc. Places of worship are named a church, chapel, grove, temple, synagogue, sanctuary, tabernacle, cathedral, mosque, etc. Officers and persons connected with sacred service are known as priest, rabbi, scribe, pope, pontiff, prelate, cure, parson, pastor, shepherd, rector, preacher, chaplain, friar, prior, abbot, vicar, abbess, monk, seer, prophet, clergy, clergyman, ecclesiastic, evangelist, apostle, minister, leader, cardinal, hermit, itinerant, colporteur, missionary, dignitary, disciple, bishop, deacon, presbyter, laity, layman, sister, father, follower, convocation, congregation, hearer, auditor, believer, member, warden, chorister, organist, precentor, singer, incumbent, archbishop, elder, clerk, etc. A theocracy is a state governed by the direction of God.

102. *Parts of a Flower and Plant.*

ca lyx	style	spa dix
se pal	bract	um bel
pe tal	pol len	cor ymb
pis til	an ther	pan i cle
sta men	o va ry	ped i cel
stig ma	co rol la	pe dun cle

103. *Divisions of Land.*

coast	cra ter	o a sis
shore	val ley	vol ca no
hill	pla teau	con ti nent
plain	isth mus	pen in su la
cape	prai rie	prom on tory
des ert	moun tain	is land

104. *Divisions of Water.*

sea	lake	creek
bay	loch	brook
gulf	mere	o cean
cove	tarn	ca nal
bight	pool	la goon
firth	pond	chan nel
in let	ford	es tu a ry

105. *Words Relating to Music.*

bar	tune	bass
clef	pitch	al to
time	sound	ten or
key	chord	so lo
note	scale	rhythm
rest	space	meas ure
beat	voice	sem i tone
tone	du et	so pra no

106. *Musical Instruments.*

fife	bu gle	gui tar
drum	cor net	pi a no
flute	cym bal	vi o lin
lute	trum pet	clar i on
vi ol	trom bone	clar i o net
ban jo	oph i cleide	tam bou rine

107. *Precious Stones.*

gem	ag ate	sap phire
jew el	o nyx	em er ald
bril liant	ber yl	di a mond
ru by	jas per	cor ne li an
o pal	gar net	am e thyst
to paz	car bun cle	mal a chite

108. *Words Used in History.*

rel ic	sub jects	pres i dent
ep och	man ners	gov er nor
bar on	cus toms	po ten tate
ty rant	count ess	roy al ty
des pot	mon arch	mon u ment
an cient	com merce	ma jes ty
mod ern	sen ate	au to crat
sa cred	gen try	min is try
peo ple	na tion	sov er eign

109. *Words Used in History.*

earl	an nals	dem a gogue
czar	fac tion	par lia ment
king	vice roy	gov ern ment
queen	scep tre	dy nas ty
count	con gress	pop u lace
duke	e vent	tyr an ny
tribe	re volt	an ar chy
horde	mis rule	au then tic
knight	na val	re bel lion
throne	peer age	dic ta tor
sol dier	pa tri ot	cit i zens

110. *Words Used in Grammar.*

verb	sub ject	in ter jec tion
noun	sen tence	con junc tion
clause	pars ing	mod i fi er
phrase	ar ti cle	a nal y sis
ad verb	el e ment	com par i son
pro noun	pred i cate	con ju ga tion
ad junct	ad jec tive	prep o si tion

111. *Words Used in Natural Philosophy.*

mass	im pact	rar i ty
force	con tact	rar e fy
space	duc tile	den si ty
dense	brit tle	grav i ty

touch	vi brate	gran u lar
weigh	ex pand	tan gi ble
tough	con tract	te nu i ty
mo tion	con dense	te na ci ty
mat ter	re volve	ve lo ci ty

112. *Words Used in Natural Philosophy.*

im pinge	re flect	po ros i ty
con verge	re tard	mag net ic
com press	ab sorb	pul ver ize
ap proach	as cend	re frac tion
co here	ad here	ex pan sion
di verge	in ten si ty	mo men tum
de scend	ra di a tion	pen e tra ble
fric tion	ca lor ic	e qui lib ri um
at tract	in verse ly	im pen e tra ble
re pel	in er ti a	in com pres si ble

113. *Studies.*

mu sic	gram mar	hy gi ene
read ing	bot a ny	ge om e try
spell ing	al ge bra	ge og ra phy
writ ing	e con o my	a rith me tic
draw ing	lan guage	book-keep ing
Greek	French	phys i ol o gy
Ger man	chem is try	Lat in

114. *Review.*

MATHEMATICS treats of quantities or magnitudes. Its parts are *arithmetic; geometry*, including *trigonometry* and *conic sections*; and *analysis*, including *algebra, analytical geometry*, and *calculus*. Some arithmetical terms are, add, subtract, more, less, multiply, divide, increase, decrease, figures, numeration, notation, Roman, Arabic, sum, amount, product, quotient, remainder, difference, compute, plus, minus, subtrahend, minuend, fraction, integer, decimal, aliquot, interest, principal, payment, equality, multiple, reduction, whole, mixed, prime, naught, insurance, proportion, percentage, problem, question, example, answer, numerator, denominator, root, cube, etc.

115. *Review.*

GEOGRAPHY treats of the world, its races of men, other animals, products, etc. Earth is our planet, globe, world, etc. Parts of land are called continent, island, isthmus, peninsula, cape, promontory, steppe, mountain, volcano, desert, oasis, plain, shore, prairie, etc. The water is divided into oceans, seas, lakes, gulfs or bays, straits, etc. The races of men are the Caucasian, Mongolian, African, and Malayan. Other words used are, city, country, town, state, province, district, archipelago, abyss, ravine, morass, typhoon, monsoon, Arctic, Pacific, Atlantic, Northern, Southern, lagoon, plateau, estuary, temperate, physical, parterre, avalanche, torrid, frigid, tropic, equator, horizon, boundary, etc.

116. *Review.*

NATURAL PHILOSOPHY treats of material objects. The centrifugal and centripetal forces are called central forces.

ATTRACTION tends to the cohesion of bodies. It is magnetic, capillary, cohesive, etc. Velocity means rate of motion. Matter may be ductile, frangible, or brittle, dense, granular, tangible, elastic, ponderous, penetrable, impermeable, incompressible, etc

117. *Review.*

HISTORY is an orderly record of the chief events which concern a people. It is known as ancient, modern, sacred, profane, general, complete, brief, abridged, etc. Historical stories, essays, anecdotes, annals, and narratives, should be authentic. Historic periods are ages, decades, epochs, centuries, etc. History describes leaders, rulers, ministers, nations, governments, states, customs, manners, seditions, rebellions, revolutions, adventures, etc.

118. *Names of Men.*

Aa ron	Am brose	Ber nard
A bel	A mos	Ber tram
A bi jah	An drew	Ca leb
Ab ner	An tho ny	Cal vin
A bra ham	Ar chi bald	Ce cil
Ad am	Ar nold	Ce phas
A dol phus	Ar thur	Charles
Al bert	A sa	Chris to pher
Al ex an der	Au gus tus	Clar ence
Al fred	Bald win	Claude
Al ger non	Bas il	Clem ent
A lon zo	Ben e dict	Cor ne li us
Al vin	Ben ja min	Cuth bert

Cyr il	Fred er ic	Job
Cy rus	George	John
Dan i el	Gid e on	Jo nas
Da vid	Gil bert	Jon a than
Don ald	God frey	Jo seph
Di o ny si us	Greg o ry	Josh u a
Dun can	Gus ta vus	Jo si ah
Eb en e zer	Guy	Ju li us
Ed gar	Har old	Jus tin
Ed mund	Hen ry	Lam bert
Ed ward	Her bert	Law rence
Ed win	Her man	Lem u el
Eg bert	Hez e ki ah	Leon ard
E li	Hi ram	Le vi
E li as	Hor ace	Lew is
E li jah	Ho ra tio	Li o nel
E noch	Hu bert	Lo ren zo
E phra im	Hugh	Lu cius
E ras tus	Hum phrey	Luke
Er nest	Hu go	Lu ther
Eu gene	I ra	Mark
Eus tace	I saac	Mar ma duke
E ze ki el	Ja bez	Mat thew
Ez ra	Ja cob	Mau rice
Fe lix	James	Mar tin
Fer di nand	Jas per	Mi chael
Fran cis	Je rome	Miles
Frank lin	Jes se	Mor gan

Mo ses	Raph a el	Sil va nus
Na than	Ray mond	Sil ves ter
Na than i el	Re gi nald	Sim e on
Nich o las	Reu ben	Si mon
Nor man	Rich ard	Sol o mon
Oc ta vi us	Rob ert	Ste phen
Oli ver	Rod er ic	Syd ney
Or lan do	Ro ger	Thad de us
Os car	Ro land	The o dore
Pat rick	Ru fus	The oph i lus
Paul	Ru pert	Thom as
Pe leg	Sam son	Tim o thy
Pe ter	Sam u el	Ur ban
Phil ip	Saul	Vin cent
Phin e as	Seth	Wal ter
Ralph	Si las	Zach a ri ah

119. *Names of Women.*

Ab i gail	Al mi ra	Au gus ta
A da	A man da	Bar ba ra
Ad e line	A me li a	Be a trice
Ad e la	A my	Be lin da
A de li a	Am a bel	Ber tha
Ag a tha	An ge li na	Bet sey
Ag nes	Ann	Blanche
Al ber ta	An na	Brid get
Al ex an dra	An nie	Car o line
Al ice	Ar a bel la	Cath a rine

Ce li a
Char i ty
Char lotte
Chris ti na
Ci ce ly
Clar a
Clar is sa
Clem en ti na
Con stance
Co ra
Cor de li a
Cor ne li a
Cyn thi a
Deb o rah
De li a
Do ra
Dor cas
Dor o thy
Dru sil la
E dith
El e a nor
El i nor
E li za
E liz a beth
El la
El len
El vi ra
Em ma

Em i ly
Em me line
Es ther
Eu ge ni e
Eu nice
Eu phe mi a
E va
E van ge line
Ev e line
Faith
Fan nie
Flo ra
Fran ces
Fred e ri ca
Ger al dine
Ger trude
Grace
Han nah
Har ri et
Hel en
Hen ri et ta
Hes ter
Hope
I da
I nez
I rene
Is a bel la
Jane

Ja net
Jo se phine
Ju dith
Ju li a
Lau ra
La vin i a
Le o no ra
Le ti ti a
Lil i an
Lil ly
Lo rin da
Lou i sa
Lu cin da
Lu cre ti a
Lu cy
Lyd i a
Ma bel
Mad e line
Mar ga ret
Ma ri a
Mar i on
Ma ry
Mar tha
Ma til da
Maud
Mel i cent
Me lis sa
Mer cy

Mil dred	Phe be	Sa rah
Min nie	Pol ly	So phi a
Mi ran da	Pris cil la	Stel la
Nan cy	Pru dence	Su san
No ra	Rachel	Vic to ri a
Ol ive	Re bec ca	Vi o la
O phe li a	Rho da	Vir gin i a
Pa tience	Ruth	Viv i an
Pau line	Sal ly	Win i fred

120. *Words Denoting Deity.*

Always begin with a Capital Letter.

God	The Fa ther	The In fi nite
Lord	The Ma ker	The E ter nal
De i ty	The Rul er	Om nip o tent
Al might y	The Cre a tor	Om ni pres ent
Je ho vah	The Pre serv er	Su preme Be ing

121. *Kinds of Birds.*

vul ture	pea cock	mag pie
con dor	pi geon	al ba tross
os trich	pheas ant	cor mo rant
e mu	wood cock	par o quet
buz zard	swal low	fla min go
par rot	hen hawk	o ri ole
pet rel	spoon bill	ca na ry

122. *Names of Flowers.*

daf fo dil	ca mel lia	cac tus
mar i gold	pe tu nia	dah li a
hy a cinth	ver be na	fuch si a
col um bine	nas tur tium	ge ra ni um
he li o trope	car na tion	mign o nette
sun flow er	dan de li on	gil ly flow er

123. *Daily Retail Market Report.*

Butter	50@60	Celery, ⅌ doz.	50@75
Honey	20@25	Radishes, do.	20@25
Eggs, hens'	30@40	Artichokes, do.	50@1.00
do. ducks'	35@45	Horseradish, do.	10@15
Lard, ⅌ lb	18@20	Mushrooms, do.	25@35
Bacon	18@25	Melons, each	48@50
Onions, ⅌ lb	1½@ 2	Peppers, do.	25@35
Caulifl'rs, each	10@15	Garlic, do.	5@ 8
Cabbages, do.	12@20	Eschalots, do.	20@25

124. *Possessives.*

goodness' sake	ladies' school	Mechanics' Institute
righteousness' sake	girls' class-room	misses' shoes
conscience' sake	boys' wardrobe	men's ideas
Moses' law	miners' strike	women's rights
Jesus' feet	joiners' tools	children's clothing
Xerxes' army	Farmers' Bank	brethren's meeting

125. *Abbreviations.*

A Gen. from Eng., a Col. from Fr., a Maj. from N. S., a Capt. from N. B., and a Lieut. from Man., visited Rt. Hon. Sir John Macdonald in Can.

Rev. Sam. Jackson, D. D., and Gov. Robinson, accompanied James Jones, Jun., Esq., M. P., to N. Y.

Mr. and Mrs. Smith, with their sons, Jno. and Jas., went to consult James E. Graham, M. D., in Tor., on the 12th of Feb.

Messrs. Brown & Co. sent 74 doz. eggs, 3 hhd. of sugar, 12 bbl. of apples, 6 cwt. 3 lb. 4 oz. of salt, on the 10th inst., by G. T. R., to Belleville.

Students may receive the degree of B. A., M. A., LL. B., LL. D., or C. E., at Univ. Coll.

Pres. Gage and Prof. Earls addressed St. James's S. S., on the 15th inst.

PART II.

Words liable to be misspelled because the same sounds in them are spelled in different ways.

1.

ain, ane, ein, eign, aign.

drain	plain	chain
swain	gain	main
ab stain	sprain	strain
crane	ap per tain	sus tain
pro fane	bane	in sane
skein	hu mane	wane
deign	ar raign	cam paign

2.

ause, aws, auze.

cause	pause	with draws
be cause	ap plause	straws
laws	draws	gnaws
flaws	squaws	gauze

3.

ald, auled, alled, awled.

bald	scald	stalled
called	mauled	crawled
squalled	sprawled	drawled

4.

all, awl, aul.

in stall	fore stall	gall
bawl	drawl	wall
sprawl	brawl	crawl
maul	haul	yawl

5.

aud, oad, awed.

fraud	de fraud	ap plaud
broad	a broad	pawed
sawed	gnawed	laud

6.

ay, ey, eigh.

bray	al lay	flay
fray	de fray	a stray
af fray	dis play	dis may
de lay	they	re pay
be tray	pur vey	ar ray
con vey	dis o bey	sur vey
o bey	weigh	in veigh

7.

eak, ake.

break	steak	make
brake	stake	flake
shake	drake	snake
a wake	spake	for sake
par take	mis take	un der take

8.

eak, eek, iek, ique.

beak	bleak	creak
freak	squeak	sneak
wreak	streak	be speak
peak	creek	meek
shriek	seek	sleek
an tique	pique	u nique
clique	ob lique	cri tique

9.

ean, een, ene, in, ine.

dean	wean	clean
lean	green	un clean
be tween	spleen	fore seen
un seen	ca reen	ob scene
con vene	se rene	ma rine
rou tine	ra vine	man da rin

10.

ear, eer, ere, ier.

sear	smear	spear
year	be smear	tear

ap pear	dis ap pear	en dear
ar rear	jeer	gear
leer	cheer	queer
sneer	ca reer	ve neer
dom i neer	mu ti neer	gaz et teer
pi o neer	ad here	co here
se vere	aus tere	gren a dier
in ter fere	per se vere	chan de lier
cav a lier	fron tier	gon do lier

11.

eat, eet, ete, eit, eipt.

bleat	heat	peat
seat	en treat	treat
de feat	re peat	re treat
re plete	con crete	com plete
fleet	greet	se crete
street	dis creet	ob so lete
con ceit	de ceit	re ceipt

12.

ease, eece, eese, iece, ice, ise.

de cease	lease	cease
re lease	de crease	in crease
fleece	va lise	a piece
geese	po lice	ca price

13.

ie, ei.

a chieve	grief	re lieve
be lieve	weird	re prieve

brief	lei sure	re trieve
chief	lief	shield
con ceit	liege	nei ther
con ceive	niece	be siege
ei ther	per ceive	shriek
liege	piece	siege
de ceit	pierce	thief
de ceive	seiz ure	tier
field	shield	wield
fiend	priest	yield
fierce	re ceive	in vei gle

14.

oan, one, own.

roan	moan	loan
hone	drone	prone
en throne	de throne	post pone
own	sown	shown
known	thrown	flown

15.

ue, eu, ieu, ui, ew, iew.

clue	few	sue
cue	is sue	tis sue
val ue	en sue	sub due
im bue	en due	ar gue
res cue	pur sue	res i due
rev e nue	un due	rue ful
neu ter	ret i nue	eu lo gy

lieu	con tin ue	a dieu
view	pur lieu	pew ter
beau ty	re view	bar be cue
jui cy	nui sance	be dew
screw	rue	con strue
threw	true	ac crue

NOTE. — Long *u* and its substitutes following the letter *r* sound like *oo* in cool; in all other cases they sound like *yu* or the word *you*.

16.

Words ending in **cy**, **sy**, *and* **zy**.

i cy	fan cy	flee cy
leg a cy	lu na cy	fal la cy
in fan cy	pri va cy	pa pa cy
pi quan cy	bril lian cy	va can cy
flu en cy	de cen cy	clem en cy
po ten cy	id i o cy	sol ven cy
ex cel len cy	di plo ma cy	cur ren cy
as cen den cy	buoy an cy	com pe ten cy
con fed er a cy	ar is toc ra cy	per sist en cy
tip sy	grea sy	po e sy
flim sy	pal sy	mass y
ea sy	gloss y	po sy
ep i lep sy	drow sy	drop sy
lep ro sy	pro sy	em bas sy
hy poc ri sy	ro sy	breez y
ha zy	brass y	maz y
cra zy	jeal ous y	ooz y
diz zy	a pos ta sy	furz y

17.

ence, ense, ents.*

sense	hence	whence
tense	com mence	dif fer ence
em i nence	dif fi dence	in di gence
in tel li gence	el o quence	in no cence
res i dence	pref er ence	ref er ence
ex cel lence	pen i tence	ve he mence
mag nif i cence	neg li gence	mu nif i cence
con dense	om nip o tence	be nef i cence
dis pense	im mense	sus pense
li cense	non sense	in cense
rec om pense	re lents	frank in cense
set tle ments	re pents	fer ments
gov ern ments	la ments	pre vents
es tab lish ments	ex per i ments	in stru ments

18.

Words ending in **eous** *and* **ious.**

pit e ous	hid e ous	lig ne ous
du te ous	vit re ous	beau te ous
plen te ous	a que ous	cu ta ne ous
os se ous	boun te ous	spon ta ne ous
sim ul ta ne ous	ex tra ne ous	ho mo ge ne ous
het e ro ge ne ous	in stan ta ne ous	cu ri ous
o di ous	du bi ous	en vi ous
stu di ous	ob vi ous	im pi ous
va ri ous	co pi ous	ca ri ous
fu ri ous	glo ri ous	se ri ous
in ju ri ous	spu ri ous	pe nu ri ous

* t should be sounded.

im pe ri ous
fe lo ni ous
ac ri mo ni ous
par si mo ni ous
de lir i ous
ab ste mi ous
cer e mo ni ous
sanc ti mo ni ous
la bo ri ous
ne fa ri ous
ig no min i ous
del e te ri ous

19.

Words ending in able and ible.

laud a ble
ten a ble
af fa ble
blam a ble
teach a ble
peace a ble
change a ble
fal li ble
pos si ble
le gi ble
for ci ble
hor ri ble
com bus ti ble
i ras ci ble
cur a ble
prob a ble
pal pa ble
port a ble
suit a ble
sal a ble
ser vice a ble
tan gi ble
vis i ble
flex i ble
ter ri ble
cor rupt i ble
in di ges ti ble
cul pa ble
du ra ble
ca pa ble
sen si ble
li a ble
laugh a ble
tax a ble
no tice a ble
ed i ble
fu si ble
fea si ble
com press i ble
ir re sist i ble
in del i ble
el i gi ble

20.

Words ending in efy and ify.

stu pe fy
ed i fy
sig ni fy
glo ri fy
fals i fy
sanc ti fy
rar e fy
pu tre fy
de i fy
vit ri fy
clar i fy
cer ti fy
li que fy
dig ni fy
ver i fy
ter ri fy
beau ti fy
fruc ti fy

am pli fy	jus ti fy	pet ri fy
dis qual i fy	in dem ni fy	per son i fy

21.

Words ending in **ety** *and* **ity**.

ni ce ty	pi e ty	so ci e ty
so bri e ty	prob i ty	anx i e ty
pro pri e ty	de i ty	im pro pri e ty
no to ri e ty	quan ti ty	brev i ty
qual i ty	en mi ty	grav i ty
suav i ty	sanc ti ty	gra tu i ty
an nu i ty	hu mil i ty	dex ter i ty
ur ban i ty	ma lig ni ty	stu pid i ty
a vid i ty	prod i gal i ty	com mod i ty
neu tral i ty	prob a bil i ty	mal le a bil i ty
tran quil li ty	fer til i ty	in cre du li ty

Reviews of Difficult Words.

1.

jeer	va lise	ca price
skein	ex hale	blas pheme
weigh	in veigh	cam paign
shriek	re ceipt	pal i sade
kneel	con ceit	ser e nade
pique	fron tier	chan de lier
e rase	cri tique	su per sede
se cede	rou tine	gaz et teer
u nique	ob scene	mas quer ade
ob lique	con ceal	gren a dier

2.

seize	grieve	re ceive
weird	sor tie	re prieve
pyre	a piece	per ceive
lurch	sur feit	a chieve
liege	for feit	sur plice
wield	lei sure	mor tise
fierce	be siege	seiz ure
shield	re lieve	ben e fit

3.

do cile	gen e sis	proph e sies
ser vile	def i nite	chrys a lis
vac cine	ret i nue	den ti frice
chas tise	civ il ize	o bei sance
pur lieu	dis ci pline	sac ri fice
nui sance	crit i cise	tyr an nize
san guine	par a lyze	mag net ize
mar line	pre ju dice	crys tal lize

4.

bruise	de vi ous	scan da lous
a dieu	stim u lus	ve he mence
gua no	symp tom	neg li gence
im brue	pre vi ous	el o quence
li cense	pen i tence	am big u ous
id i om	vig i lance	il lus tri ous
nau ti lus	rec om pense	pre ca ri ous

5.

trea cle	blam a ble	tech ni cal
cap tious	teach a ble	bril lian cy

fea si ble	de cen cy	i ras ci ble
tax a ble	peace a ble	in del i ble
sal a ble	buoy an cy	el i gi ble
i ci cle	priv i lege	change a ble
cyn i cal	pi quan cy	ser vice a ble
chem i cal	poig nan cy	sym met ri cal

6.

schism	triv i al	fil ial
gnome	cai tiff	de sign
cir cuit	pan nier	pe cu li ar
pur suit	rai ment	com plex ion
val iant	cinc ture	pe cu ni a ry
pur loin	debt or	crys tal line
ha rangue	dis guise	lab y rinth
hyp o crite	ma lign	guar an tee

7.

spe cial	in i tial	per sua sion
nup tial	sa ti ate	de lir i ous
cau tious	vi ti ate	ne go ti ate
con scious	stu di ous	far i na ceous
rem e dy	scar ci ty	ab ste mi ous
tra ge dy	vil la ny	hy poc ri sy
tyr an ny	jeal ous y	lieu ten an cy
pit e ous	het er o ge ne ous	min strel sy

PART III.

Words pronounced alike, or nearly alike, but spelled differently, with different meanings.

NOTE. — It is thought best not to give lists of these words with their meanings, as pupils may get them in their dictionaries, if the *connection in which the words are used* does not enable the pupils to decide their meaning.

For review purposes, or to save time, teachers may read the sentences, emphasizing the words in *italics*, and the pupils may write these words only. The order in which they are written will enable the teacher to test their accuracy.

Lesson I.

The *air* will be cold *ere* morning. Did you *e'er* see the *heir* to the estate? What can *ail* the man? He has drunk too much *ale*. *All* shoes are sewed with an *awl*. They are going to *alter* the *altar* of the church. My *aunt ate* an *ant* at *eight* o'clock. You never *ought* to do *aught* without your father's *assent*. The *ascent* was steep. The teacher *bade* me beware of *bad* men. The man *bawled* when the *ball* struck him on his *bald* head. A *bard* is a poet. The gay *belle*, having *rung* the *bell* for a light, *barred* the door and retired. He could not *bear* to have the *bear* bite his *bare* leg. As the *bier passed* she thought of the *past* and *wrung* her hands with anguish. I have *been* to the corn *bin*. He *brews* good *beer*. I have a *bruise* on my hand. The girl asked her *beau* to *buy* her a pink *bow*. As he went *by* he said, "Good by."

Lesson II.

The *bough* of the tree made the man *bow*. His *birth* took place in a *berth* of the vessel. A well-*bred* young man held the horse's *bridle* while the *bridal* party got a loaf of *bread* and a *bowl* of milk. The *beech*-tree near the ocean *beach* has a large *bole*. A *Briton* is a native of *Britain*. What a large *berry*! *Bury* the poor *brute*, and do not *bruit* about his faults. The wind *blew* the clouds across the *blue* sky. Put the *bait* on the hook. Do you know your *lesson*? To *bate* means to *lessen*. Look at the *calendar*, and see the date. *Calender* the cloth. A *chaste* woman was *chased* by a *cruel* man, and dropped a ball of *crewel*. Cats *climb* with their *claws*. Read the first *clause* of the sentence. The ships and their *crews* are in a foreign *clime* on a *cruise*. The parcel, *tied* with a *coarse cord*, floated on the *tide*. Of *course* you will take the classical *course*. Sound a *chord* on the organ.

Lesson III.

I shall *canvass* the country for subscribers. The *counsel* for the accused appeared before the *council*, which met in a *canvas* tent. The *colonel* served in the Sixth *Corps*. The apple was found to be rotten at the *core*. The fine city of

Washington is the *capital* of the U. S., and its finest building is the *Capitol*. *Canon* Kingsley fired a *cannon*. The *cession* of Alaska to the U. S. was made during the *session* of Congress. The *choleric* man wore a paper *collar*. Don't try to *cozen* me, my *cousin*. While I was *sealing* my letter, a spider dropped from the *ceiling* of the room. The *seller* of tickets is in the *cellar*. He *sent* me the *cent* he *owed* me for the *ode* I wrote. The *scent* of the flower is sweet. It is a good *site* for a house, and commands a fine *sight* of the ocean. I will *cite* a passage of Scripture. I want a *quire* of paper for the *choir*. My shoes *creak*. The *cygnet* is swimming in the *creek*. Have you my *signet* ring?

Lesson IV.

The *coward cowered* before me. A lady should not *choose* a man who *chews* tobacco. He bought a *currant* pie for ten cents *current* money. If you *desert* your friends at dinner, you will get no *dessert*. My *dear*, did you see the *deer* in the park? It was a *doe*. Bakers *knead* the *dough* with their hands; we *need* bread to eat. He had *done* his work and was ready to *die*. *Dye* the cloth a *dun* color. *Oh!* how I dislike to *dun* people for money they *owe* me, even after it is *due!* *Dost* thou not see that the *dust* is wet with *dew?* A *dire* calamity befell the *dyer* on the sea. Do you *see* the *ewe* under the *yew*-tree? Take *exercise* every day, to *exorcise* the spirit of laziness. The vase is shaped like an *urn*. I will *hire* a man who can *earn higher* wages. Do not *faint* away; the attack was only a *feint*. Home is a sacred *fane*, which I would *fain* keep pure. Never *feign* sickness because you do not *know* your lesson. Dare to say, *No*.

Lesson V.

The *fair* lady has paid her *fare*. We had good *fare* at the *fair*. The horse is lame in the right *fore* foot. The gymnast performed a wonderful *feat*. The stick is *four feet* long The man went *forth* to kill a *fowl*. That was *foul* play. He succeeded the *fourth* time The barrel of *flour* rolled over a *flower*. *Flocks* of birds ate the *phlox* seed. *Jane* bought ten yards of blue *jean*. She walked with an easy *gait through* the *gate*, as if unconscious of *guilt*. The boy *threw* a stone. The *gilder made* a *gilt* frame worth a *guilder* for the pretty *maid*. The *great* man sat by the open *grate*, and *sighed* that he was not *greater*. His dog is by his *side*. Have you a nutmeg *grater?* I would rather *meet* a *grizzly* bear than a *grisly* ghost. It is *meet* that we should eat *meat*. He will *mete* out justice.

Lesson VI.

The bat *flew* up the chimney *flue*. The ox *gored* the cow. I struck him with a *gourd*. The *grease* was sent to *Greece*. My *guest guessed* the riddle. Bad men *gamble* with cards; lambs *gambol* in the field. The *hale* old man was out in the *hail*. *Haul* the load to the *hall*. The *hare* is a kind of *rabbit*. The carpenter made a *rabbet* in the *board*. I was *bored* by the foolish talk. The *hair* of the *holy* man is *wholly* white. I showed *him* the *hymn*. He bought ten feet of gutta-percha *hose*. I bought two steel *hoes*. The jury will *indict* the man for theft. The teacher will *indite* this sentence. He laid *our* book on the table. He has *lain* in the *lane* an *hour*. I came *here* to *hear* the lecture

Lesson VII.

A man of *lax* principles *lacks* character. You can tell a *mean man* by his sneaking *mien*. A *male* friend brought my *mail* from the office. Lumbering is the *main* business in *Maine*. He held the horse's *mane* with all his *might*. A widow's *mite* may have a *mighty* influence. The lord of the *manor* has a dignified *manner*. He wears a fur *mantle*. The parlor *mantel* is made of marble. Do you like *martial* music? The *marshal rode* a horse of high *mettle* along the *road*, and wore a *metal* badge. Do not *meddle* with my gold *medal*. The *mower mowed* the field once *more* in the best *mode*. The *mucous* membrane secretes *mucus*. *Gneiss* makes a very *nice* window-sill. Do not *mewl* like a baby; the *mule* will not hurt you. The *mist* was so dense that I *missed* sight. The *nun* could find *none*. The man carried silver *ore o'er* the bridge on the *oar* of the boat. The girl who carried the *pail* looked *pale*.

Lesson VIII.

One boy *won* a *prize*. He never *pries* into other people's business. He suffers *pain*. Who broke that *pane* of glass? It is *plain* that the *plane* is dull. In geometry we speak of *planes*; in geography, of *plains*. There is a wide *plait* in her dress. The *plate* is on the table. The Christian *prays* to God and sings his *praise*. The hawk *preys* upon other birds. A *pallet* is a bed, and a *palette* is a painter's board. Good food gratifies the *palate*. He tried to *pare* the *pear* with a *pair of* scissors. "Let us have *peace*," not war. He ate a *piece* of lemon *peel*. Did you hear that *peal* of thunder? When he gets over his *pique* we shall be friends again. The English *peer* climbed the *peak* of the mountain. The ship is at the *pier*. A lawyer who makes good *pleas* is sure to *please* his clients.

Lesson IX.

Will you have a *plum?* That pole does not stand *plumb.* Exercise opens every *pore* of the skin. Please to *pour* me a glass of water. Do not *pore* over your books so much. The *Principal* said, "Our men of *principle* should be our *principal* men." Put your foot upon the *pedal.* Those who *peddle* make a good *profit.* Isaiah was a great *prophet.* I have a piece of *pumice*-stone. There is *pomace* at the cider mill. Gold is found in *quartz* rock. Four *quarts* make a gallon. He drives with a tight *rein.* Hear it *rain.* The *reign* of Victoria is prosperous. To tear down is to *raze.* My *son* says, "We cannot *raise* corn without the *rays* of the *sun.*" He *read* till his eyes were *red.* In the Bible we *read* of a bruised *reed.*

Lesson X.

Write to the wheel*wright.* Do *right.* The pastor administered the *rite* of baptism. Milton *wrote* "Paradise Lost." Do not recite by *rote.* The *wretch* got sick and began to *retch.* Forty rods make a *rood.* Do not be *rude* and *rough* in your behavior. She wears a *ruff.* He tasted the *rye* bread and made a *wry* face. I have just *seen* a beautiful *scene.* I bought canvas at a *sale* to make a *sail* for the boat. He made a *slight* mistake in his *sleight* of hand. The wild *surge* wrecked the boat. Buy me ten yards of *serge. Sew* the seam *so. Sow* the seed early. He tried to *steal* a *steel* pen. He has lost the *sole* of his shoe. The *soul* is immortal.

Lesson XI.

The ship is a fast *sailer,* and has a good *sailor* for captain. The fisherman caught a *sucker.* Always *succor* the distressed. Irving's *style* is much admired. "I'm sitting on the *stile*, Mary." The cross and crown are sacred *symbols*. He plays the *cymbals* in the band. The *tale* is too true. The squirrel has a bushy *tail*. I want some 6 oz. *tacks*. I pay no *tax* when I *travel* in Europe. The *throes* of *travail* are severe. The bad boy *throws* stones at the birds. He *threw* the ball *through* the window. It is *too* bad *to* make *two* mistakes in one word. They went *there* and got *their* books. The *throne* was *thrown* down. "They went and *told* the sexton, and the sexton *tolled* the bell."

Lesson XII.

Improve your *time*. *Thyme* grows in the garden. There is a gilded *vane* on the steeple. He has ruptured a *vein*. Do not be *vain* of your acquirements. The *vial* contains poison. He plays upon the *viol*. Can you *wade* across the river? Come this *way*. *Wait* till I get *weighed*. How much do you *weigh*? My *weight* is 140 lbs. That girl has a small *waist*. Do not *waste* your time. He keeps good *wares*. She *wears* a dress a *week*. I feel *weak*. The *wether* suffers during the cold *weather*. The *yoke* is of *wood*. I *would* like to have the *yolk* of an egg. Long may our flag *wave* o'er the ocean *wave*. I *waive* my right to exemption.

Review.

If you should e'er have to submit to the ordeal of a searching examination in English orthography, you should ere going up make yourself thoroughly acquainted with an air of confidence and an heir at law, your Aunt Hill and the anthill in the copse, a beefsteak and a gambler's stake, an elective or hereditary peer and a stone pier, tears of joy and tiers of seats, beer for the living and a bier for the dead, the base of a pyramid and the bass of an anthem or a hymn. Learn the difference between him who wields the adze and him who ever adds to his wealth; between the Bey of Tunis and the Bay of Naples, the bays of Europe and the green baize table-cover, the graceful boughs of the beech and the swelling bows of the boat on the beach, or the polite bows of the beau bending like a bow; between the feminine belle and a brass bell, a policeman's beat and a vegetable beet, the bight of a rope and the bite of a rattlesnake, the birth of a child and the berth of a sailor, the breech of a gun and the breach which the lätter makes in a wall, a broach for a roast and a brooch for a lady, a rabbit burrow and a municipal borough, a brass cannon and an ecclesiastical canon, a cession of territory and a session of Parliament, the cord of a whip and the chord of a fiddle, the dough in a kneading-trough and the doe in the forest, a cattle-fair and a cab or omnibus fare, a school-fellow and the felloe of a wheel. All such words demand the learner's special attention, if he wishes to avoid the ludicrous blunders of those who write hairbrained for harebrained, bearfaced and bearfooted for barefaced and barefooted, pole-tax for poll-tax, plumline for plumbline, raindear for reindeer, duclap for dewlap, tailbearer for talebearer.

PART IV.

Words liable to be misspelled.

Every teacher should keep lists of the words misspelled by his pupils. The pupils themselves should keep at the back of their dictation and composition books lists of the words they spell incorrectly.

The following lists serve as a review of the whole book, and contain some additional words. They may be used for spelling-matches or for examinations.

Lesson 1.

abyss	anodyne	arena
adept	acquiesce	although
abridge	aggregate	affright
assuage	allopathic	abdicate
acrostic	antipathy	abeyance
anchovy	accuracy	abrogate
apathy	accelerate	abstinence
ancestry	acme	acoustic
amateur	athlete	assignee
aversion	avouch	analogous

Lesson 2.

apoplexy	anthracite	arraign
anonymous	adipose	acquaint
apostrophize	amalgam	adieu
abstruse	arabesque	allege
athwart	aborigines	airy
almanac	athenæum	author
abnormal	annexation	awning
absolute	aught	achieve
abutment	asked	autumn
accomplice	awed	almonds

Lesson 3.

ankles	altar	already
almost	anguish	artifice
ague	afghan	admittance
auger	arctic	advertise
always	although	attorney
apiece	allspice	aqueous
accede	allegiance	alienate
assess	alias	associate
abscess	acquittal	audible
adhere	abetted	amiable

Lesson 4.

ascendant	architect	analysis
æsthetic	ascension	association
asbestos	aqueduct	archæology
apparel	abstinence	accordion
apothegm	apostasy	apothecary

alcohol asparagus alligator
almanac bagatelle begrudge
beguile bronchitis bohea
burlesque bigamy bulwark
business bulletin brunette

Lesson 5.

bargain bright balk
burglary blight biscuit
buffalo brought buying
barren bough bequeath
boudoir brief baptize
buoyant basque bereave
bourgeois breadth bunion
banditti blonde bosom
behavior bruise benzine
bight balm bristles

Lesson 6.

benumb bazaar blamable
brooches burgher betrayer
bouquet benign barytone
benefit baboon business
bilious buggy busily
bureau blazing beauteous
bodice balance benignant
believe brazen barbecue
banian beleaguer beastliness
bawble beautify bananas

Lesson 7.

catechise
callous
caboose
calm
creosote
calumet
colloquy
cognizance
climax
careen

cavalry
clerical
commissary
capillary
chivalric
caprice
crevasse
calumny
cartilage
calisthenics

compasses
clothe
chief
crutch
chintz
chyle
chyme
calk
craunch
chord

Lesson 8.

clique
cough
chamois
canard
conceit
canoe
canteen
camphene
colic
crochet

currants
cousin
captious
conscious
chestnut
chloral
conceive
conscience
chignon
champagne

charade
crevice
coerce
caucus
chastise
canker
cipher
Christmas
crotchet
camphor

Lesson 9.

cigar
chagrin
chapel
copy
carriage

campaign
catarrh
cologne
christen
chalky

coiffure
chenille
chemise
critical
coercion

chasten	condemn	colonize
cupboard	carbine	concurred
couple	chlorine	calico
chorus	coffee	chocolate
chronic	catchup	cameo

Lesson 10.

cabbages	conciliate	counterfeit
colonel	civilian	cleanliness
creator	cinchona	charlatan
coalesce	chandelier	cochineal
courier	clumsiness	cinnamon
cordial	cynical	crystalline
copier	chemistry	chrysalis
chicory	chivalry	coruscation
covetous	colonnade	caligraphy
consequence	cordially	confectionery

Lesson 11.

cotyledonous	changeable	commissariat
cauliflower	cinnamon	corruptible
caoutchouc	curable	criticise
chameleon	cupola	courage
connoisseur	courageous	chargeable
chloroform	constellation	debris
doughty	derrick	dwarf
defraud	double	douche
dilemma	default	dredge
depth	dulcimer	distaff

Lesson 12.

drudge	deceit	data
debut	dahlia	dispel
defile	dairy	deceive
deluge	diary	debauch
dynasty	dollar	detach
dight	dyeing	ductile
dough	dungeon	diamond
drought	demesne	dwindle
disk	depot	dizzily
daughter	duet	duteous

Lesson 13.

dialogue	discretion	domineer
dynamics	dysentery	domicile
devious	divisible	derision
diaphragm	diarrhœa	diurnal
despondent	deficiency	daguerrotype
debonair	dromedary	eulogist
ensconce	effervesce	Eolian
epiglottis	eccentric	equipage
eulogy	episode	etymology
elapse	edge	eighth

Lesson 14.

eagle	embalm	exertion
efface	editor	ecstasy
erase	epistle	edifice
extreme	epitaph	efficient
esquire	euphony	etiquette

eyot
exhaust
exhort
enroll
expel
exchequer
erasable
evident
essential
elegant
exorbitant
exhaustible
expatiate
enterprise
erysipelas

Lesson 15.

emissary
exhilarate
flaunt
franchise
fresco
foliage
fuse
feign
fright
fraught
extirpate
etymology
facile
fracas
falchion
fricassee
fight
flight
forte
fierce
effervescence
façade
forceps
flambeau
freight
feudal
feud
feod
furnace
fluxions

Lesson 16.

faucets
fi[illegible]
fulfil
foretell
facial
fledgeling
foreign
flippant
felon
freckle
forehead
fiendish
fifthly
furlough
fifteenth
flourish
fractious
fiasco
fussiness
fascinate
fertilize
flimsier
fuchsia
frontispiece
February
flat-iron
flexibility
fatiguing
factious
frolicsome

Lesson 17.

farinaceous	filibuster	frolicking
guide	gnaw	growth
gouge	gnawed	giant
guileless	gnarl	grieve
gulch	gnarled	gauge
gyves	gnash	grief
geyser	gnat	gauze
gazelle	gneiss	gout
glacier	gnome	gibe
gossamer	ghost	guile

Lesson 18.

gondolier	gnomon	gaiters
grown	gymnast	gracious
guise	gauger	guinea
glebe	gable	gluey
gaunt	guidance	giraffe
guy	grotesque	gherkin
goal	gopher	gristle
gallon	gingham	ghastly
grammar	good by	gusto
greasy	gratis	gypsum

Lesson 19.

gorgeous	granary	guttural
grand	gaseous	gutta-percha
gazette	glycerine	genealogy
grievous	guerilla	gorilla
guardian	ghostliness	guano

gayly	hydropathic	habituate
heinous	hippodrome	halcyon
hemorrhage	hydraulic	hominy
heterogeneous	harlequin	homœopathy
hypochondriac	height	high

Lesson 20.

halves	hoeing	hyacinth
haughty	heifers	heaven
heirship	hyphen	hygiene
handsome	hazard	hosiery
hatchet	hurried	historic
hyson	hideous	handkerchief
hymen	heresy	hecatomb
hogshead	hospital	hurricane
heaven	heinousness	hypocrite
hinging	howitzer	hibernal

Lesson 21.

hypocrisy	hymeneal	huckleberry
herbaceous	humiliate	homœopathic
homogeneous	hypercriticism	island
irony	intelligible	instil
irrigate	isolate	immense
indigenous	infallible	isthmus
ivory	ineffable	icicle
isosceles	innocence	impious
inflammation	innocuous	intercede
inoculate	ineligible	inveigle

Lesson 22.

irrigation	irrevocable	infusoria
immortelle	indictment	irrelevant
initial	inexorable	impressible
inveigh	italicize	ignis fatuus
initiate	indebted	jocular
jeopardy	jealousy	journeys
jaguar	juiciness	judgment
juicy	jeopardize	Jehovah
jilt	joyous	joking
kaleidoscope	knock	knell

Lesson 23.

kernel	knew	kangaroo
know	knead	knuckle
knave	knee	knowledge
knoll	knout	kerchief
knot	knell	kerosene
knit	knives	kleptomania
knight	kraal	knife
linguist	loathe	latchet
lymphatic	lynx	logarithm
languid	lynch	light

Lesson 24.

lozenge	lily	lettuce
liquidate	liege	lyrics
leviathan	lens	lacquer
language	luncheon	lief
laugh	lava	ledger

lease
lyre
lapse
lieu
league
luscious
loosen
leisure
loiter
laving
larynx
leopard
leper
leprosy
laudanum

Lesson 25.

livelihood
likelihood
lachrymose
literal
legacy
macaroni
metallurgy
morphine
menagerie
maintain
liquefy
Liliputian
Leviticus
ludicrous
marine
myrtle
malice
mortise
miniature
mischief
loquacious
liniment
lineament
lieutenant
might
myth
missed
mirth
model
mawkish

Lesson 26.

meagre
maiden
melon
mortgage
mantle
measles
mosaic
meerschaum
martyr
mattress
mistiness
mosquito
medicine
manuscript
molasses
malfeasance
marmalade
mistletoe
merino
maximum
moccason
moneyless
marriageable
movable
machinery
mahogany
metempsychosis

Lesson 27.

mechanic	masquerade	normal
mackerel	manageable	nephew
nominee	nymph	nankeen
nuisance	niche	nickel
nugget	naughty	now-a-days
necessary	neighbor	nauseous
nigh	mignonette	nasturtium
naught	naphtha	nationality
nought	neuter	onslaught
niece	notation	orchestra

Lesson 28.

omelet	obscene	orchestral
ordeal	orphan	orifice
orthoepy	oyster	orator
oxalic	official	obstacle
obsequies	oscillate	officer
ornithology	obsequious	onions
ought	opera	opaque
ooze	phase	parachute
Pleiades	pierce	pneumatics
psychology	phrase	prude

Lesson 29.

paroxysm	palace	plover
pyrotechnic	porridge	puzzle
pontoon	perceive	patient
phlegm	precede	prorogue
plague	proceed	prairie

porcelain
partial
precious
programme
pigeon

poultice
python
peasant
pappoose
pheasant

package
pittance
primer
pedler
pennon

Lesson 30.

phantom
pamphlet
poignant
parasol
particle
pleurisy
polyglot
plaintiff
paradise
paroquet

piano
piety
paralyze
pinnacle
psalmody
palaver
pavilion
proselyte
putrefy
proboscis

prettily
provincial
peaceable
pitiful
porphyry
panacea
prosody
pyramid
physician
potatoes

Lesson 31.

penniless
policy
purchasable
physiognomy
politician
philologist
paralysis
quadrille
quintessence
quoits

participle
predecessor
promissory
pharmacopœia
pharmaceutical
petition
piazza
quotation
qualms
quorum

piteous
privilege
parable
psaltery
pneumonia
payable
quackery
quotient.
quinine
quartette

Lesson 32.

reindeer
retrieve
reservoir
rhomb
rogue
realm
rouge
rye
rescind
redoubt

rejoice
recollect
regalia
rhomboid
rhymer
rennet
ripple
rummage
riddance
rueful

rescue
rosette
right
rascal
raccoon
ruffian
roughen
rations
referred
rain-gauge

Lesson 33.

reigneth
routine
raisins
rhubarb
recruit
receipt
review
radius
reprieve
rebel

roguish
regime
recreant
reckoner
rheumatic
rhapsody
rhetoric
rendezvous
revenue
restaurant

raspberries
recipe
resistance
regimen
regatta
rudiment
rhinoceros
receivable
reminiscence
recourse

Lesson 34.

sycophant
synonym
spermaceti
sibylline
seethe

salad
sachem
strychnine
scythe
seized

smoulder
souvenir
synopsis
sleuth
sphinx

sight	skein	scheme
sigh	sylvan	squad
sought	sued	shrewd
slough	shield	swath
straight	sheath	sheik

Lesson 35.

siege	seraph	sturgeon
scout	sulphur	selvage
sylph	stylish	shekel
steppe	sobriety	suction
shove	stampede	schooner
spoonful	symptom	squander
scruple	sprightly	shrivel
sluice	slaughter	surfeit
sheriff	satyr	sugar
sceptre	serene	stomach

Lesson 36.

sausage	satchel	siren
sibyl	spectre	spicy
squint	species	salmon
soluble	slyly	sapphire
stirrup	sardine	sassafras
squirrel	singeing	sauciness
shepherd	scholars	serenade
surgeon	simoom	supersede
skilful	sultriness	secrecy
seizing	shovelling	surcingle

Lesson 37.

sidereal	steadiest	sovereign
subaltern	sedition	scintillate
strategic	scandalize	symmetry
soprano	solemnize	satellite
somersault	saltpetre	syllogism
stimulus	sorghum	synagogue
silhouette	survey	suicidal
sycamore	scissors	scenery
separate	silicate	siliceous
succession	salary	suspicion

Lesson 38.

synecdoche	saccharine	superstitious
serviceable	subterranean	saleratus
sybarite	soliloquy	tariff
twelfth	thwart	tapestry
trachea	tissues	tongue
thigh	twirl	though
tight	touch	tryst
taught	taunt	trawl
thought	thyme	thorough
through	thief	traitor

Lesson 39.

tortoise	toughen	terrific
tether	tonnage	traceable
tying	toilet	towelling
tartar	triple	tranquillize

trousers	trestle	typical
triphthong	tenon	tapioca
thievish	thistle	tranquillity
typhus	tonsil	tomahawk
typhoid	trisyllable	toothache
utensil	ugliest	umbrella

Lesson 40.

unique	usury	uvula
vacillate	vehicle	vertical
vineyard	vexatious	versatile
veil	veranda	ventilate
vein	vermilion	version
valet	vermicelli	victualler
vicious	vying	wight
vowel	wield	weight
wrench	weird	wrought
worth	writhe	waltzed

Lesson 41.

wrapped	wholly	wizard
whey	women	Wednesday
wrist	wrangle	wretched
wreath	wainscot	weevil
wreathe	wigwam	wrestle
wrath	wholesome	whooping
wreak	wryness	wheelwright
whistling	yeoman	yearning
zouave	zoology	zinc

TEST REVIEWS,

CONTAINING DIFFICULT WORDS.

Lesson 1.

A *chasm* in a rock. The *chord* of a musical instrument. *Chrome* is one of the metals. *Chyle* is separated from *chyme.* The *Chaldee* language. The *chloride* of lime. *Chlorine* is one of the constituents of common salt. The *chlorate* of potash. *Choler,* or anger. *Choral* symphonies. By what name will he *christen* the child? He has a disagreeable *chronic* disease. A *Chaldaic* idiom. A *chaotic* mass. A *chimera* of the imagination. A *choleric* disposition. The nations of *Christendom.* The *chromatic* scale. A faithful *chronicler* of events. The *chrysalis* of the silkworm. *Chrysolite* is a green mineral. *Chalybeate* waters contain iron. The changing hues of the *chameleon.* A *chimerical* project. His *chirography* is bad The *chiropodist* removes corns from the feet. The *chronometer* is an exact timepiece. He is subject to the *headache* A wild *scheme.*

Lesson 2.

The *addition* of numbers. Boundless *ambition.* Rocks are worn by the *attrition* of the waves. The period of *dentition* A *flagitious* action. An *initial* letter. The enrolment of *militia.* A *monition,* or warning. *Nutritious* food. In danger of *perdition.* *Propitious* circumstances The *solstitial* colure. An act of *volition.* The *accession* of Victoria to the throne of England. The *aggression* of an enemy. The *ascension* of a balloon. The *compression* of the air. *Concus-*

sion of the brain. The *discussion* of a question. The *omission* of bank bills. An idiomatic *expression*. The effect of *perversion*. The *possession* of property. A long *procession*. *Secession* from a party. The *suppression* of intemperance. *Transgression* of the law

Lesson 3.

The *caption*, or arrest of a criminal. A *captious* disposition. A *faction*, or political party. A *fractious* child. A *lotion* for a wound. *Martial* law. A *nuptial* ceremony. Be *patient*. What is the *quotient?* A soldier's *ration*. A *sentient* being. The force of *suction*. *Ablution*, or the act of washing. A strange *assertion*. A good *citation*. A *convention* of delegates. The *credentials* of an ambassador. He gave a vivid *description*. Write the exercise from my *dictation*. An *equation* in algebra. Industry is *essential* to success. *Facetious* conversation. He is *impatient* of control. The British *legation* at Washington. The *potential* mood. *Prudential* considerations. The *pulsation* of the heart. The *refraction* of light. He ate to *repletion*. He was allowed to *satiate* his appetite. A *contentious* style. A *substantial* foundation. A man's *vocation*

Lesson 6.

A *petulant* disposition. A *postulate*, or assumed position. *Saturate* the sponge with water. *Sinuous* paths. A reward to *stimulate* ambition. *Tabulate* the results. *Titular* dignities. *Tremulous* with emotion. A mortar to *triturate* minerals. *Tortuous* [illegible]. An *adventurous* spirit. An [illegible] expression. *Articulate* your words distinctly. Be *assiduous* in the pursuit of knowledge. Burgoyne was obliged to *capitulate*. *Deciduous* trees. Men sometimes seek refuge for their own *emolument*. An *estuary*, or arm of the sea. What can *extenuate* his guilt? He is fond of *horticulture* He allowed no temptations to *infatuate* him. An *ingenuous* disposition. Crafty men know how to *insinuate* what they dare not say directly. The *manumission* of a slave. An exhibition of *statuary*. A *tumultuous* rabble.

Lesson 5.

A *stanchion* under the beam of a ship. A *truncheon*, or staff. A *marchioness* is the wife of a marquis. An *avalanche* of snow. A *capuchin*, or Franciscan friar They felt great *chagrin* at their failure. A *chaise* has two wheels. *Champagne* is a sparkling wine. A *champaign*, or flat, open country. A *chandelier* for a parlor. Do you know the meaning of the *charade?* He is a base *charlatan*. A *chevalier*, or knight. A zigzag ornament in architecture is called a *chevron*. He was guilty of *chicanery* In the days of *chivalry* A *galoche*, or overshoe. Skilled in *machinery*. Does he wear a *mustache?* He showed great *nonchalance*. A *parachute* for support in the air.

PART V.

The words in the following lists were compiled from lists of "words commonly misspelled," sent from many schools in different parts of Canada. In cases of words having the same sound but different meanings, only one is given here except in a few instances. In spelling such words it is an excellent practice to ask the pupils to write sentences containing both words properly used. (See Part III.) These lists, and the words in the lists of words misspelled by the pupils themselves (Part VI.) should be used frequently for exercises in oral as well as written spelling.

aborigines
abyss
accede
accept
accordion
accommodate
achievement
accumulate
accurate
ache
acknowledgment
acquiesce
acquainted
acquittal
acoustic

amassed
amateur
ambiguous
ameliorate
amethyst
analogy
analysis
anarchy
anatomical
ancient
angels
annihilate
anodyne
anonymous
antique

archangel
architect
archives
arctic
artificial
ascent
ascertain
assailants
assassin
asphalt
assiduous
assuage
asthma
astronomy
atheism

acres
across
addition
adhere
adjoin
affability
aghast
agile
aggrieve
aisle
alcohol
allege
alley
alpaca
anxiety
aperture
apology
apoplexy
apostle
apparent
apostrophe
appalling
apparel
appearance
appellation
apprehension
aqueduct
aqueous
attachment
alphabet
audible
authority
auger
augur
author
autocrat
autumn
auxiliary
avenue
avoirdupois
awkward
axiom

bailiff
ballad
balmy
banana
bargain
barouche
battalion
bayonet
bazaar
beau
beauteous
beleaguerers
believe
benefactor
beneficent
beverage
bias
bicycle
bier
biennial
bilious
billiards
biscuit
brilliant
bivouac
bivouacked
blamable
blanc-mange
bleach
bludgeon
brethren
bridle
bridal
brigadier
Briton
Britain
Britannia
bronchitis
brooch
bruise
bureau
burial
burlesque
busiest
busily

beneficial
besieging
bevel
bachelor
borough
bosom
bounteous
balance
business
buoy
buy
bonus

calendar
calmly
caprice
cameo
campaign
camphor
cancel
captain
carat
caress
carouse
carriage
cashier
catalogue
catastrophe
catarrh
cayenne
cedar
ceiling
celestial
celery
cemetery
census
centennial
centre
chilblain
chimney
chintz
chirography
chisel
chloroform
choir
cholera
choral
chord
chorister
chronometer
cipher
circuitous
citadel
civilities
civilise
clerical
clique
coalition
cocoa
codicil
coerce
chieftain
coincide
conscience
conscientious
conscious
consent
consignee
consolatory
convalescent
conveyance
coolly
coquette
coral
corpuscle
corpse
cough
cuisine
councillor
counterfeit
coupon
courier
courtesy
cowardice
crescent
cried
crisis
critical

cereals
ceremonies
chagrin
chalk
chamois
chandelier
changeable
chaise
chaos
charade
chastisement
chasm
chattel
cheerily
cheque
chestnuts

colonel
column
cohesive
coming
commercial
committee
committing
comparing
compel
conciliate
conducive
conical
concealed
concede
congenial
conqueror

criticism
crooked
crochet
crocodile
croquet
crucify
cruising
crystallize
cupboard
curiosity
cycle
cyclone
cymbal
cynical
cypress
czar

dilapidated
defendant
dilemma
donkey
disguise
digit
dairy
diary
divine
discern
disburse
discipline
dulcimer

dishonor
demagogue
diminutive
demeanor
diphtheria
deference
diagnose
deficit
descendant
dandelion
dispense
defalcation
dungeon

disappear
description
despair
decide
discomfited
dissolve
dispossessed
disposable
desperate
dependent
dulness
development
debarred

deity
diphthong
derision
dutiful
disease
despatch
dissipate
delirious
disciple
daguerreotype
detachment
derogatory
diffuse
dictionary
digestible
docile

eligibility
embezzle
erroneous
efficacy
expense
efficiency
existence
enemies
errand
extraordinary
entrance
excellent
enrolment
echoing
embarrassing
emerge
eminent
examiner
execrable
eccentricities
elegy
envelope
excursion
essential
eager
economy
explicit
either
epitome
enormous
eyrie
electrician
equilibrium
emaciate

fuchsia
frigid
facsimile
furry
forehead
fertilise

facile
financier
feign
fiend
fractious
furlough
falcon
falchion
felony
foliage
fete

frontier
feud
financial
fiery
faucet
facilitate
friend
fledged
fumigate
February
fibres

forcible
fascinate
ferocious
fulfil
familiar
finally
fissure
frivolous
feint
foreign
fibrous

gauge
guarantee
graphic
guardian
guinea
gingham
ghostly
glossary
glazier
guttural
gratuitous
grammar

gnash
giraffe
gnat
granary
gaudy
geranium
gymnastics
gnaw
gypsy
guitar
glisten
gases

gorgeous
grateful
group
gluttonous
grievous
ghastly
grandeur
guillotine
gasolier, gasalier
galleries
guest
grenadier

havoc
heinous
hydraulic
hypothesis
hymn

heresy
hallelujah
hyacinth
hosiery
hazard

hostler
height
hurriedly
heroic
haughty

harangue
history
hoeing
homœopathy
honeysuckle
hyena
heifer
hickory
hieroglyphics
hydrophobia
hyphen
hygiene
hemorrhage
hypocrisy
hideous
huge
harassing
hoarse
hippopotamus
hiccough
humorous
hoping
hilarious
hue
hoard
hierarchy
handkerchief

illegible
inaudible
indict
isthmus
inseparable
impetuous
incredible
irresistible
isolate
illicit
ivy
inveigle
intercede
irrepressible
initial
iron
iota
impatient
irretrievable
immense
incense
install
impromptu
incision
icicle
impassible
interred
imagine
indigestible
infidels
intensely
immerse
imminent
imaginary
image
idols
itself
independent
invincible
ingenuous
intrigue
issuing
interrogatory
insidious
imitate
implement
inflammatory
island
interfere
innocuous
indispensable
incandescent
indebtedness
indefinite

jovial
jeopardy
jeweller

jaundice	judgment	jealousy
juicy	janitor	joining
jostle	journey	joust
kleptomaniac	knap-sack	knotty
kyle	knolls	knows
kiln	knives	knocks
knuckle	knavery	knowledge
knell	knelt	kernel
laughter	locomotive	licorice
linen	lathe	larynx
lichen	lapel	label
loitered	launch	liquor
lozenge	luncheon	lose
loose	larceny	losing
liege	lattice	lizard
license	lettuce	lieutenant
luscious	lynx	length
levelled	leisure	lustre
linguist	leopard	ludicrous
loathe	lion	liniment
lilies	lacerate	lovable
machinery	mercenary	morsel
missile	muscle	mysteries
miscellaneous	mahogany	mournful
malady	mayor	maintaining
mortice	municipal	multiple
minion	mimicking	musing
malice	myriad	monarchs

WORDS OFTEN MISSPELLED.

morgue	mignonette	martyrs
[illegible]	mutinous	meant
[illegible]	melancholy	metre
melodious	massacre	miniature
marriage	mortgage	moisten
medal	mechanic	mien
myrtle	mosquito	mighty
[illegible]	menagerie	moustache
mistletoe	murmur	monetary
mackerel	magnificent	mountainous
monosyllable	model	meteor
[illegible]	metal	martial
meridian	manœuvre	musician
[illegible]	mischievous	moneys
negotiate	nausea	nervous
neuralgia	naphtha	naughty
neutral	necessarily	nutritious
[illegible]	niece	nucleus
[illegible]	nominative	nineteenth
niche	neighbor	naval
nickel	nephew	nitre
opulent	opaque	ordinarily
ordinance	oriole	ought
o'clock	obloquy	orchestra
ocular	optician	opposite
orifice	obsequies	owes
onyx	occurrence	oyster
obeisance	orphan	oblique
[illegible]	opportunity	once

oscillate	operation	odor
onion	occurred	opium
ostrich	omitted	ocean
oxygen	occasions	officious

precision	picnicking	polygamy
preparation	presence	pickerel
pursuit	parallelogram	potential
pagan	pretence	pedagogue
perennial	perceptible	phosphate
precise	pneumatic	Presbyterian
precede	pore	persuade
privilege	pyramids	principle
phonography	pencilled	pleasant
pedal	poem	particle
plaid	pistols	prodigious
participle	prophetic	propagate
placid	periodicals	police
plausible	pompous	parachute
persistence	portrait	precipice
pitiable	patient	prairie
passion	piazza	porridge
paradise	piteous	precious
phaeton	palatial	piece
palate	porcelain	poison
perseverance	phenomenon	peasantry
porpoise	phrenology	precincts
pancreas	parliament	precocious
physiology	psalm	prescience
palpable	pleurisy	pressure

piety	phlegm	plebeian
preferred	physique	process
pneumonia	plenteous	piano
petroleum	paroxysm	picture
prestige	plateau	pitcher
paralysis	phantom	precedent
pharmacy	porous	patriarch
purify	parochial	palm
poultice	pier	phrase
practice	poor	pewter
practise	pernicious	peculiar
pronunciation	penitentiary	priests
quite	quarrel	querulous
quiet	quotient	quartz
quorum	qualm	quest
quinine	queen	query
rouge	remittance	recruit
[illegible]	ruffian	rhetoric
rhythm	rarefy	reprieve
receive	reservoir	refrigerator
recompense	ratio	raisin
razor	rendezvous	restaurant
[illegible]	radical	rhapsody
rhubarb	rhyme	rain
reiterate	recognise	rescind
[illegible]	reformatory	ravenous
[illegible]	rolled	resources
[illegible]	reception	reverential

recommend
resistance
remembrance
repetition
ridiculous
reconcile
receipt

recipe
ridge
resplendent
required
rhinoceros
refulgent
route

receding
revellers
response
religious
reign
raspberries
reconnoitre

sieve
sacrilege
sumach
supercede
skeleton
stereotype
sluice
skein
surname
schedule
susceptible
suite
senior
separate
scuttle
sagacious
swindle
sycamore
shovel
specimen
syllable
suasion

sauce
similar
sure
sterile
sensible
soldier
shoulder
splendor
slender
stretched
salubrious
sepulchre
scimitar
sacrilegious
sacrifice
severe
sulphur
siphon
symbol
supremacy
sandwich
sirloin

stomach
synthesis
salable
symmetry
sovereign
spontaneous
silhouette
saturday
smooth
succor
sleight
shrewd
sense
stencil
soiree
strychnine
sanctioned
substantially
stationary
sewer
sealed
shining

sinew
spigot
seizing
specie
sanguine
suspense
superficial
souvenir
suitable
sleeve
skilfully
sickness
[illegible]
sloping
stirring
satirical
serviceable
[illegible]
siege
speech

shield
scrofula
sausage
scissors
synonymous
steak
surcingle
subtle
salmon
stereoscope
synonym
subpoena
sturgeon
singeing
stupefy
sergeant
sardine
soliloquy
sylvan
sapphire

sceptre
said
sword
spinach
sweat
scholars
sincere
solemn
sphere
satchel
shriek
sequel
salary
surplus
surplice
succeed
sonorous
sugar
sympathy
speedily

turbulence
tuition
tacit
telegraph
truly
traitor
tyrant
truant
telephone

tortoise
tranquillity
tantalize
typhus
theatres
thieving
talents
torture
terrace

tassels
tenacious
thoroughly
twelfth
treacle
thought
touch
trouble
tongue

tomato	terrier	threw
tomahawk	threshold	tailor
trivial	territories	tenant
troche	toothache	traveller
trestle	trisyllable	tremendous
trespass	tureen	trapeze
triennial	tentacles	too, to, and two
tyranny	treacherous	tragedy
triphthong	typhoid	tableau

until	unchangeable	uneasily
unparalleled	union	unrobing
undeniable	undoubted	universal
unskilful	umbrella	utility
using	unsuccessful	unanimous

villain	valleys	voice
village	volume	vigilant
violence	various	visible
variegated	voluble	vizier
vacillating	view	volition
voracious	victuals	verdure
valise	veins	vigorous
vertical	virtue	vassal
vegetable	vehicle	vicious
valiant	vermicelli	virtually
vengeance	victualler	very

wrestle	wizard	wilful
waltz	woollen	wondering

wield	wholly	writing
wrinkle	witnessed	worshipped
whistle	Wednesday	wrapped
wily	wretch	whose
weapon	women	wharf
yolk	yeoman	yeast
yield	yawl	yew
yacht	yearn	yesterday
zealous	zephyr	zoology

PART VI.

Additional list of common words liable to be misspelled, written under the direction of the teacher.

PART VII.

Literary Selections.

The selections in Part VII. are intended to be *memorized* and *recited*, as well as used as *dictation lessons*.

In making these selections two objects were kept in view: the inculcation of *good moral lessons* and *literary* merit.

Instead of using the recitation hour for the improvement of a few pupils who *least* require to be trained in the practice of the principles of elocution, thoughtful teachers are uniformly learning the importance of assigning lessons in recitation, as in all other subjects, to all the members of a class. The advantages of such a course are very many. Among these may be named the following:—

1. Every pupil has his mind stored in early years with a collection of the choicest gems of the literature of his language.

2. As all the pupils have prepared the same lesson, each one is able intelligently to take part in the study of the selections in school with a view to their proper recitation.

3. Pupils can recite simultaneously as well as individually.

4. The memories of all the pupils will be cultivated by the practice.

Studying the lessons for dictation, and writing them as dictation lessons, will aid in committing them to memory.

The ability to recite a certain number of appropriate selections should be one of the tests for promotion from one class to another.

Selections suitable for Pupils in the Second Reader.

1.

Our Father who art in heaven, hallowed be thy name. Thy kingdom come. Thy will be done on earth, as it is in heaven. Give us this day our daily bread: and forgive us our trespasses, as we forgive them that trespass against us. And lead us not into temptation, but deliver us from evil; for thine is the kingdom, and the power, and the glory, for ever. Amen. — *Matt.* vi. 9–13.

2.

I. Thou shalt have no other gods before me.

II. Thou shalt not make unto thee any graven image, or any likeness of anything that is in heaven above, or that is in the earth beneath, or that is in the water under the earth: thou shalt not bow down thyself to them, nor serve them: for I the Lord thy God am a jealous God, visiting the iniquity of the fathers upon the children unto the third and fourth generation of them that hate me; and showing mercy unto thousands of them that love me, and keep my commandments.

III. Thou shalt not take the name of the Lord thy God in vain; for the Lord will not hold him guiltless that taketh his name in vain.

IV. Remember the Sabbath day, to keep it holy. Six days shalt thou labor, and do all thy work: but the seventh day is the Sabbath of the Lord thy God: in it thou shalt not do any work, thou, nor thy son, nor thy daughter, nor thy man-servant, nor thy maid-servant, nor thy cattle, nor thy stranger that is within thy gates: for in six days the Lord made heaven and earth, the sea, and all that in them is, and rested the seventh day: wherefore the Lord blessed the Sabbath day, and hallowed it.

V. Honor thy father and thy mother: that thy days may be long upon the land which the Lord thy God giveth thee.

VI. Thou shalt not kill.

VII. Thou shalt not commit adultery.

VIII. Thou shalt not steal.

IX. Thou shalt not bear false witness against thy neighbor.

X. Thou shalt not covet thy neighbor's house, thou shalt not covet thy neighbor's wife, nor his man-servant, nor his maid-servant, nor his ox, nor his ass, nor anything that is thy neighbor's. — *Exod.* xx. 3–17.

3.

Then one of them, which was a lawyer, asked him a question, tempting him, and saying,

Master, which is the great commandment in the law?

Jesus said unto him, Thou shalt love the Lord thy God with all thy heart, and with all thy soul, and with all thy mind.

This is the first and great commandment.

And the second is like unto it, Thou shalt love thy neighbor as thyself.

On these two commandments hang all the law and the prophets. — *Matt.* xxii. 36–40.

4.

And seeing the multitudes, he went up into a mountain: and when he was set, his disciples came unto him:

And he opened his mouth, and taught them, saying,

Blessed are the poor in spirit: for theirs is the kingdom of heaven.

Blessed are they that mourn: for they shall be comforted.

Blessed are the meek: for they shall inherit the earth.

Blessed are they which do hunger and thirst after righteousness: for they shall be filled.

Blessed are the merciful: for they shall obtain mercy.

Blessed are the pure in heart: for they shall see God.

Blessed are the peacemakers: for they shall be called the children of God.

Blessed are they who are persecuted for righteousness' sake: for theirs is the kingdom of heaven.

Blessed are ye, when men shall revile you, and persecute you, and shall say all manner of evil against you falsely, for my sake.

Rejoice, and be exceeding glad: for great is your reward in heaven; for so persecuted they the prophets which were before you. — *Matt.* v. 1–12

5.

Beautiful faces are they that wear
The light of a pleasant spirit there;
It matters little if dark or fair.

Beautiful hands are they that do
Deeds that are noble, good, and true;
Busy with them the long day through.

Beautiful feet are they that go
Swiftly to lighten another's woe,
Through summer's heat or winter's snow;

Beautiful children, if, rich or poor,
They walk the pathways safe and pure,
That lead to the mansion strong and sure.

6.

Do your best, your very best,
And do it every day;
Little boys and little girls,
That is the wisest way.

Whatever work comes to your hand,
At home, abroad, at school,
Do your best with right good will,
It is a golden rule

7.

If you find your task is hard,
Try, try again;
Time will bring you your reward
Try, try again;
All that other folks can do,
Why, with patience, should not you?
Only keep this rule in view:
TRY, TRY AGAIN

8.

Do all the good you can,
In all the ways you can,
To all the people you can,
Just as long as you can.

9.

A word may part the dearest friends, —
 One little, unkind word,
Which in some light, unguarded hour
 The heart with anger stirred.

A look will sometimes send a pang
 Of anguish to the heart:
A tone will often cause the tear
 In sorrow's eye to start.

One little act of kindness done,
 One little kind word spoken,
Hath power to make a thrill of joy
 E'en in a heart that 's broken.

10.

Only a drop in the bucket,
 But every drop will tell;
The bucket soon would be empty,
 Without a drop in the well.

Only a poor little penny, —
 It was all I had to give;
But as pennies make the dollars,
 It may help some cause to live.

God loveth the cheerful giver,
 Though the gift be poor and small;
What does he think of his children
 When they never give at all?

11.

'T is *being*, and *doing*,
 And *having*, that make
All the pleasures and pains
 Of which beings partake.

To *be* what God pleases,
  To *do* a man's best,
And *to have* a good heart,
  Is the way to be blest. — *Peter Parley.*

12.

"I Can't" is a sluggard, too lazy to work;
From duty he shrinks, every task he will shirk;
No bread on his board and no meal in his bag;
His house is a ruin, his coat is a rag

"I Can" is a worker; he tills the broad fields,
And digs from the earth all the wealth that it yields;
The hum of his spindle begins with the light,
And the fires of his forges are blazing all night.

13.

Hearts, like doors, can ope with ease
  To very, very little keys;
And don't forget that they are these:
  "I thank you, sir," and, "If you please."

Then let us watch these little things,
  And so respect each other;
That not a word, or look, or tone,
  May wound a friend or brother.

14.

Dare to be honest, good, and sincere,
Dare to please God, and you never need fear.

Dare to be brave in the cause of the right,
Dare with the enemy ever to fight.

Dare to be loving and patient each day,
Dare speak the truth whatever you say.

Dare to be gentle and orderly too,
Dare shun the evil, whatever you do.

Dare to speak kindly, and ever be true,
Dare to do right, and you 'll find your way through.

15.

Count that day lost
  Whose low descending sun
Views from thy hand
  No worthy action done

16.

Be good, my friend, and let who will be clever;
  Do noble things, not *dream* them all day long,
And so make life, death, and that *vast forever*,
  One grand, sweet song

17.

I live for those who love me,
  For those who know me true,
For the heaven that smiles above me,
  And awaits my spirit too;
For the cause that lacks assistance,
For the wrong that needs resistance,
For the future in the distance,
  And the good that I can do.

18.

Over and over again,
  No matter which way I turn,
I always find in the book of life
  Some lesson that I must learn;
I must take my turn at the mill,
  I must grind out the golden grain,
I must work at my task with a resolute will,
  Over and over again.

19.

Dare to do right! dare to be true!
The failings of others can never save you;
Stand by your conscience, your honor, your faith,
Stand like a hero, and battle till death.

20.

Do what conscience says is right;
Do what reason says is best;
Do with all your mind and might;
Do your duty, and be blest.

21.

Speak gently, kindly, to the poor;
Let no harsh term be heard;
They have enough they must endure,
Without an unkind word. — *David Bates.*

22.

I count this thing to be grandly true,
That a noble deed is a step toward God,
Lifting the soul from the common sod
To a purer air and a broader view. — *J. G. Holland.*

23.

A little word in kindness spoken,
A motion, or a tear,
Has often healed the heart that's broken,
And made a friend sincere.

A word — a look — has crushed to earth
Full many a budding flower,
Which, had a smile but owned its birth,
Would bless life's darkest hour.

Then deem it not an idle thing
  A pleasant word to speak;
The face you wear, the thoughts you bring,
  A heart may heal or break. — *Colesworthy.*

24.

Within this ample volume lies
The mystery of mysteries;
Happiest they of human race
To whom their God has given grace
To read, to fear, to hope, to pray,
To lift the latch, to force the way;
And better had they ne'er been born,
That read to doubt, or read to scorn.

Walter Scott.

25.

Thou truest friend man ever knew,
  Thy constancy I 've tried;
When all were false, I found thee true,
  My counsellor and guide.
The mines of earth no treasures give
  That could this volume buy;
In teaching me the way to live,
  It taught me how to die. — *George P. Morris.*

26.

"No God! no God!" The simplest flower
  That on the wild is found
Shrinks as it drinks its cup of dew,
  And trembles at the sound.
"No God!" astonished Echo cries
  From out her cavern hoar;
And every wandering bird that flies
  Reproves the atheist lore.

27.

If men were wise in little things,
  Affecting less in all their dealings, —
If hearts had fewer rusted strings
  To isolate their kindly feelings, —
If men, when Wrong beats down the Right,
  Would strike together and restore it, —
      If Right made Might
      In every fight, —
  The world would be the better for it. — *W. H. Cobb.*

28.

A mother's love, how sweet the name!
  What is a mother's love?
A noble, pure, and tender flame,
  Enkindled from above,
To bless a heart of earthly mould, —
The warmest love that can grow cold, —
  This is a mother's love. — *Montgomery.*

29.

He prayeth well who loveth well
  Both man and bird and beast;
He prayeth best who loveth best
  All things, both great and small;
For the dear God, who loveth us,
  He made and loveth all — *Coleridge.*

30.

Rest not! Life is sweeping by,
Go and dare before you die;
Something mighty and sublime
Leave behind to conquer time;
  Glorious 't is to live for aye,
  When these forms have passed away — *Goethe*

31.

For God has marked each sorrowing day,
  And numbered every secret tear,
And heaven's long years of bliss shall pay
  For all his children suffer here. — *W. C. Bryant.*

32.

Beware the bowl! though rich and bright
Its rubies flash upon the sight,
An adder coils its depths beneath,
Whose lure is woe, whose sting is death.
Alfred B. Street

Selections for Classes in the Third Book.

1.

God hath a presence, and that you may see
In the fold of the flower, the leaf of the tree;
In the sun of the noonday, the star of the night;
In the storm-cloud of darkness, the rainbow of light;
In the waves of the ocean, the furrows of land;
In the mountain of granite, the atom of sand;
Turn where you may, from the sky to the sod,
Where can ye gaze that ye see not a God? — *Eliza Cook*

2.

The quality of mercy is not strained,
It droppeth as the gentle rain from heaven
Upon the place beneath: it is twice blest;
It blesseth him that gives and him that takes:
'T is mightiest in the mightiest: it becomes
The throned monarch better than his crown:
It is an attribute to God himself,

And earthly power doth then show likest God's
When mercy seasons justice. Consider this,
That, in the course of justice, none of us
Should see salvation: we do pray for mercy;
And that same prayer doth teach us all to render
The deeds of mercy. — *Shakespeare.*

3.

We live in deeds, not years, — in thoughts, not breaths, —
In feelings, not in figures on a dial; —
We should count time by heart-throbs. He most lives
Who thinks most, — feels the noblest, — acts the best.

Bailey.

4.

God moves in a mysterious way,
His wonders to perform;
He plants his footsteps in the sea,
And rides upon the storm.

Deep in unfathomable mines
Of never failing skill,
He treasures up his bright designs,
And works his sovereign will.

Ye fearful saints, fresh courage take;
The clouds ye so much dread
Are big with mercy, and shall break
In blessings on your head. — *Cowper.*

5.

Judge not the Lord by feeble sense,
But trust him for his grace;
Behind a frowning Providence
He hides a smiling face.

His purposes will ripen fast,
  Unfolding every hour;
The bud may have a bitter taste,
  But sweet will be the flower.

Blind unbelief is sure to err,
  And scan his work in vain;
God is his own interpreter,
  And he will make it plain. — *Cowper.*

6.

Press on ! surmount the rocky steeps;
  Climb boldly o'er the torrent's arch;
He fails alone who feebly creeps,
  He wins who dares the hero's march.
Be thou a hero! let thy might
  Tramp on eternal snows its way;
And through the ebon walls of night
  Hew down a passage unto day.

7.

The heights by great men reached and kept
  Were not attained by sudden flight,
But they, while their companions slept,
  Were toiling upward in the night. — *Longfellow.*

8.

Nothing is greater sacrilege than to prostitute the great name of God to the petulancy of an idle tongue. — *Jeremy Taylor.*

9.

The Devil tempts men through their ambition, their cupidity, or their appetite, until he comes to the profane swearer, whom he catches without any reward. — *Horace Mann.*

10.

The foolish and wicked practice of profane cursing and swearing is a vice so mean and low, that every person of sense and character detests and despises it. — *George Washington.*

11.

Who is thy neighbor? He whom thou
Hast power to aid or bless;
Whose aching head or burning brow
Thy soothing hand may press.

Thy neighbor is the fainting poor,
Whose eye with want is dim;
O, enter then his humble door
With aid and peace for him.

Thy neighbor? Pass no mourner by;
Perhaps thou canst redeem
A breaking heart from misery; —
Go, share thy lot with him.

12.

A cheerful temper, joined with innocence, will make beauty attractive, knowledge delightful, and wit good-natured. It will lighten sickness, poverty, and affliction, convert ignorance into an amiable simplicity, and render deformity itself agreeable. — *Addison.*

13.

God is glorified, not by our groans, but our thanksgivings; and all good thought and good action claim a natural alliance with good cheer. — *E. P. Whipple.*

14.

To be happy, the passions must be cheerful and gay, not gloomy and melancholy. A propensity to hope and joy is real riches; one to fear and sorrow, real poverty. — *Hume.*

15.

Lying 's a certain mark of cowardice ;
And when the tongue forgets its honesty,
The heart and hand may drop their functions, too,
And nothing worthy be resolved or done

Thomas Southern.

16.

Work ! and pure slumbers shall wait on thy pillow ;
Work ! thou shalt ride over care's coming billow.
Lie not down wearied 'neath woe's weeping willow,
Work with a stout heart and resolute will !
Work for some good, be it ever so slowly ;
Work for some hope, be it ever so lowly ;
Work ! for all labor is noble and holy ! — *Mrs. Osgood.*

17.

We count the Scriptures of God to be the most sublime philosophy. I find more marks of authenticity in the Bible than in any profane history whatever. — *Isaac Newton.*

18.

The Bible contains more true sublimity, more exquisite beauty, more pure morality, more important history, and finer strains of poetry and eloquence, than can be collected from all other books, in whatever age or language they have been written. — *Sir William Jones.*

19.

Life should be full of earnest work,
Our hearts undashed by fortune's frown :
Let perseverance conquer fate,
And merit seize the victor's crown.
The battle is not to the strong,
The race not always to the fleet ;
And he who seeks to pluck the stars
Will lose the jewels at his feet. — *P. Cary.*

20.

Sweet clime of my kindred, blest land of my birth!
The fairest, the dearest, the brightest on earth!
Where'er I may roam, howe'er blest I may be,
My spirit instinctively turns unto thee!

21.

In the world's broad field of battle,
  In the bivouac of Life,
Be not like dumb, driven cattle!
  Be a hero in the strife!

Trust no Future, howe'er pleasant!
  Let the dead Past bury its dead!
Act, — act in the living Present!
  Heart within, and God o'erhead.

Lives of great men all remind us
  We can make our lives sublime,
And, departing, leave behind us
  Footprints on the sands of time; —

Footprints that perhaps another,
  Sailing o'er life's solemn main,
A forlorn and shipwrecked brother,
  Seeing, shall take heart again.

Let us, then, be up and doing,
  With a heart for any fate;
Still achieving, still pursuing,
  Learn to labor and to wait. — *Longfellow.*

22.

At evening to myself I say,
Where hast thou been and gleaned to-day, —
  Thy labors how bestowed?
What hast thou rightly said or done?
What grace attained, and knowledge won,
  In following after God? — *Charles Wesley.*

23.

Words of kindness we have spoken
May, when we have passed away,
Heal, perhaps, a spirit broken,
Guide a brother led astray. — *J. Hagen.*

Speak gently! 't is a little thing,
Dropped in the heart's deep well;
The good, the joy, that it may bring,
Eternity shall tell. — *D. Bates.*

24.

Though waves and storms go o'er my head,
Though strength, and health, and friends be gone;
Though joys be withered all and dead,
And every comfort be withdrawn:
On this my steadfast soul relies, —
Father, thy mercy never dies. — *Wesley.*

25.

Thou art, O God, the life and light
Of all this wondrous world we see;
Its glow by day, its smile by night,
Are but reflections caught from thee.
Where'er we turn, thy glories shine,
And all things fair and bright are thine.
Thomas Moore.

26.

Hours are golden links, God's token,
Reaching heaven; but one by one
Take them, lest the chain be broken
Ere thy pilgrimage be done.
Adelaide A. Procter.

27.

O God! that men should put an enemy in their mouths to steal away their brains! — *Shakespeare.*

28.

The habit of using ardent spirits by men in office has occasioned more injury to the public and more trouble to me than all other causes. And were I to commence my administration again, the first question I would ask respecting a candidate for office would be, "Does he use ardent spirits?"

Thomas Jefferson.

29.

Greatness of any kind has no greater foe than a habit of drinking. — *Walter Scott.*

30.

Those are the great of earth, —
Great not by kingly birth,
Great in their well-proved worth,
  Firm hearts and true. — *J. Pierpont.*

31.

Temperance and labor are the two best physicians of man; labor sharpens the appetite, and temperance prevents him from indulging to excess. — *Rousseau.*

32.

Work for the good that is nighest;
  Dream not of greatness afar;
That glory is ever the highest
  Which shines upon men as they are.
Work, though the world would defeat you;
  Heed not its slander and scorn;
Nor weary till angels shall greet you
  With smiles through the gates of the morn.

W. M. Punshon.

33.

True worth is in being, not seeming, —
In doing each day that goes by
Some little good, not in dreaming
Of great things to do by and by;
For, whatever men say in their blindness,
And spite of the fancies of youth,
There is nothing so kingly as kindness,
And nothing so royal as truth.

Alice Cary.

34.

The rose, which in the sun's bright rays
Might soon have drooped and perished,
With grateful scent the shower repays
By which its life is cherished:
And thus have e'en the young in years
Found flowers within that flourish,
And yield a fragrance fed by tears,
That sunshine could not nourish.

Bernard Barton.

35.

One by one the sands are flowing,
One by one the moments fall;
Some are coming, some are going;
Do not strive to grasp them all.

One by one thy duties wait thee,
Let thy whole strength go to each;
Let no future dreams elate thee, —
Learn thou first what these can teach.

Adelaide A. Procter.

Selections for Classes in Fourth and Fifth Books.

1.

We rise by things that are 'neath our feet;
  By what we have mastered of good and gain;
  By the pride deposed, and the passion slain,
And the vanquished ills that we hourly meet

J. G. Holland.

2.

It may not be our lot to wield
The sickle in the ripened field,
Nor ours to hear on summer eves
The reaper's song among the sheaves,
Yet where our duty's task is wrought
In unison with God's great thought,
The near and future blend in one,
And whatsoe'er is willed is done. — *Whittier.*

3.

There's a wideness in God's mercy
  Like the wideness of the sea;
There's a kindness in his justice,
  Which is more than liberty.
For the love of God is broader
  Than the measure of man's mind;
And the heart of the Eternal
  Is most wonderfully kind — *F. W. Faber*

4.

The fairest action of our human life
  Is scorning to revenge an injury.
For who forgives, without a further strife,
  His adversary's heart to him doth tie.
And 'tis a firmer conquest, truly said,
  To win the heart, than overthrow the head

Elizabeth Carew

5.

The day is drawing to its close,
And what good deeds, since first it rose,
  Have I presented, Lord, to thee?
What wrongs repressed, what rights maintained,
What struggles passed, what victories gained,
What good attempted and attained,
  As offerings of my ministry? — *Longfellow.*

6.

Be wise to-day; 't is madness to defer;
Next day the fatal precedent will plead;
Thus on, till wisdom is pushed out of life.
Procrastination is the thief of time;
Year after year it steals, till all are fled,
And to the mercies of a moment leaves
The vast concerns of an eternal scene — *Young.*

7.

Whene'er a noble deed is wrought,
Whene'er is spoken a noble thought,
  Our hearts in glad surprise
  To higher levels rise.
The tidal wave of deeper souls
Into our inmost being rolls,
  And lifts us unawares
  Out of all meaner cares. — *Longfellow.*

8.

Truth, crushed to earth, shall rise again;
  The eternal years of God are hers:
But Error, wounded, writhes with pain,
  And dies among his worshippers. — *Bryant.*

9.

Speak gently to the erring: O, do not thou forget,
However darkly stained by sin, he is thy brother yet!
Heir of the selfsame heritage, child of the selfsame God,
He hath but stumbled in the path thou hast in weakness trod.

F. C. Lee.

10.

Rouse to some work of high and holy love,
And thou an angel's happiness shalt know, —
Shalt bless the earth while in the world above:
The good begun by thee shall onward flow
In many a branching stream, and wider grow;
The seed, that in these few and fleeting hours
Thy hands unsparing and unwearied sow,
Shall deck thy grave with amaranthine flowers,
And yield thee fruits divine in heaven's immortal bowers.

C. Wilcox.

11.

The lesson which the many-colored skies,
The flowers, and leaves, and painted butterflies,
The deer's branched antlers, the gay bird that flings
The tropic sunshine from its golden wings,
The brightness of the human countenance,
Its play of smile, the magic of a glance,
For evermore repeat,
In varied tones and sweet,
That beauty, in and of itself, is good. — *Whittier.*

12.

I would not waste my spring of youth
In idle dalliance; I would plant rich seeds
To blossom in my manhood, and bear fruit
When I am old. *J. A. Hillhouse.*

13.

Let us be patient! These severe afflictions
  Not from the ground arise,
But oftentimes celestial benedictions
  Assume this dark disguise.

We see but dimly through the mists and vapors;
  Amid these earthly damps,
What seem to us but sad, funereal tapers
  May be heaven's distant lamps. — *Longfellow*

14.

No man is born into the world whose work
Is not born with him; there is always work,
And tools to work withal, for those who will;
And blessed are the horny hands of toil.

J. R. Lowell.

15.

There 's nothing bright, above, below,
From flowers that bloom to stars that glow,
But in its light my soul can see
Some feature of thy Deity!

There 's nothing dark, below, above,
But in its gloom I trace thy love;
And meekly wait that moment, when
Thy touch shall turn all bright again.

Thomas Moore.

16.

The Lord is my shepherd; I shall not want.

He maketh me to lie down in green pastures: he leadeth me beside the still waters.

He restoreth my soul: he leadeth me in the paths of righteousness for his name's sake.

Yea, though I walk through the valley of the shadow of death, I will fear no evil: for thou art with me; thy rod and thy staff they comfort me.

Thou preparest a table before me in the presence of mine enemies: thou anointest my head with oil; my cup runneth over.

Surely goodness and mercy shall follow me all the days of my life: and I will dwell in the house of the Lord forever. — *Psalm* xxiii.

17.

Take heed that ye do not your alms before men, to be seen of them: otherwise ye have no reward of your Father which is in heaven.

Therefore when thou doest thine alms, do not sound a trumpet before thee, as the hypocrites do in the synagogues and in the streets, that they may have glory of men. Verily I say unto you, They have their reward.

But when thou doest alms, let not thy left hand know what thy right hand doeth:

That thine alms may be in secret: and thy Father which seeth in secret himself shall reward thee openly.

And when thou prayest, thou shalt not be as the hypocrites are: for they love to pray standing in the synagogues and in the corners of the streets, that they may be seen of men. Verily I say unto you, They have their reward.

But thou, when thou prayest, enter into thy closet, and when thou hast shut thy door, pray to thy Father which is in secret; and thy Father which seeth in secret shall reward thee openly.

But when ye pray, use not vain repetitions, as the heathen do: for they think that they shall be heard for their much speaking.

Be not ye therefore like unto them: for your Father knoweth what things ye have need of, before ye ask him. — *Matt.* vi. 1–8.

18.

Be kindly affectioned one to another with brotherly love; in honor preferring one another;

Not slothful in business; fervent in spirit; serving the Lord;

Rejoicing in hope; patient in tribulation; continuing instant in prayer;

Distributing to the necessity of saints; given to hospitality.

Bless them which persecute you: bless, and curse not.

Rejoice with them that do rejoice, and weep with them that weep.

Be of the same mind one toward another. Mind not high things, but condescend to men of low estate. Be not wise in your own conceits.

Recompense to no man evil for evil. Provide things honest in the sight of all men.

If it be possible, as much as lieth in you, live peaceably with all men.

Dearly beloved, avenge not yourselves, but rather give place unto wrath: for it is written, Vengeance is mine; I will repay, saith the Lord.

Therefore if thine enemy hunger, feed him; if he thirst, give him drink: for in so doing thou shalt heap coals of fire on his head.

Be not overcome of evil, but overcome evil with good. *Rom.* xii 10–21.

PART VIII.

ETYMOLOGY.

PREFIXES.

Exercises on the primary and secondary meanings of derivatives formed by Prefixes.

The pupils should be required to write similar examples under each of the prefixes.

Anglo-Saxon Prefixes *(arranged alphabetically)*.

Prefix.	Meaning.	Derivatives.	Literal Meaning.	Secondary Meaning.
a	at or on	aground	on ground	stranded—stopped
		ahead	at the head	forward - further on
be	to make	beguile	to use guile	to [illegible] — to deceive
	about	beset	to set about	to [illegible]
	by or in	below	in a lower place	inferior in rank
en	to make	ennoble	to make noble	to elevate — to exalt
	in or into	embalm	to put in balsam	to preserve

Prefix.	Meaning.	Derivatives.	Literal Meaning.	Secondary Meaning.
for	*not*	forsake	not to seek	to leave—to abandon
fore	*before*	forerunner	one who runs before	a herald—messenger
mis	*ill* or *wrong*	mislay	to lay in a wrong place	to lose
out	*above* or *beyond*	outpost	a place beyond the camp	a picket or guard
over	*above, too much*	overshadow	to place a shadow over	to shield—to protect
un	*not*	unmanly	not manly	cowardly—mean
under	*beneath*	underhand	beneath the hand	sly, or clandestine
with	*from*	withhold	to hold from	to hinder, or prevent

Classic Prefixes *(arranged alphabetically)*.

Latin.				
a, ab *or* abs	*from*	absolve	to loose from	to pardon
		abjure	to swear away from	to abandon
ad, ac, af, al, an, ap *or* ar	*to*	advance	to move to the van	to promote—to improve
		affiance	to give faith to	to promise in marriage
		apply	to fold to	to use—to ask
ante	*before*	ante-chamber	a chamber before the chief one	a waiting room
circum	*around*	circumvent	to come round another	to cheat
con, co, col, com *or* cor	*together*	concourse	a running together	a multitude
		connive	to wink together	to overlook a fault
		coincide	to fall in together	to agree

PREFIX.	MEANING	DERIVATIVES	LITERAL MEANING	SECONDARY MEANING
contra, counter	*against*	contraband	against the proclamation	smuggled
		counteract	to act against	to hinder
		counterfeit	to make against	to imitate — to feign
de	*down* or *from*	decide	to cut down	to end—to settle
		deviate	to go from the way	to err—to stray
dis or di	*apart*	disturb	to put a crowd asunder	to stir—to agitate
		dilapidation	stones falling apart	ruin—decay
e, ex or ec	*out of*	expedite	to take the feet out	to hasten or quicken
		eccentric	out of the centre	odd—peculiar
		educate	to lead out	to train — to instruct
extra	*beyond*	extravagant	wandering beyond	wasteful—wild
in, im, il or ir	*in, on,* or *into*	indorse	to write on the back	to sign—to agree
		inspect	to look into	to examine
		impede	to put the feet in	to hinder
inter	*between*	intercourse	to run between	fellowship—communication
intro	*within*	introduce	to lead within	to make acquainted
ob, oc, of, op, &c.	*against* or *in way of*	object	to throw against	to find fault
		occur	to run in way of	to happen — to appear
		offer	to put in way of	to present — to give
per	*through*	perish	to go through	to die—to wither
		perennial	through the year	lasting—perpetual
post	*after*	postpone	to place after	delay
pre	*before*	premature	before ripe	too soon, or hasty
pro	*forth* or *forward*	project	something thrown forward	a plan, or scheme

Prefix.	Meaning.	Derivatives.	Literal Meaning.	Secondary Meaning.
re	*back* or *again*	redeem reform	to buy back to form again	to save to improve — to amend
retro	*backwards*	retrograde	to step backward	to become worse
se	*aside* or *from*	secede seduce	to go aside to lead from	to leave to corrupt — to deprave
sine	*without*	sinecure	without care	an office without service
sub, suc, suf *or* sup	*under*	submit succor	to send under to run under	to yield — to resign to help — to aid
super *or* sur	*above* or *over*	superfluous superlative survive	flowing over carried above to live over	abundant — needless highest — best to remain
trans tra, traf *or* tres	*across* or *beyond*	translate traduce traffic trespass transcend	to bear across to lead across to make across to pass across to climb beyond	to interpret — to express in the words of another language to slander to trade to sin to excel
ultra	*beyond*	ultramontane	beyond the mountain	foreign
Greek.				
a *or* an	*without*	apathy anarchy	without feeling without rule	coldness confusion
amphi *or* ambi	*both sides* or *two*	amphitheatre ambiguous	theatre on both sides driving two ways	ground sloping upwards all round doubtful — uncertain
ana	*up, back* or *through*	anathema analyze	placed up to loose back	devoted — a curse to solve — to examine thoroughly
anti *or* ant	*against* or *opposite to*	antidote antarctic	given against opposite to arctic	a cure for poison — a remedy

Prefix	Meaning	Derivative	Literal Meaning	Secondary Meaning
apo or aph	from	apologize	to reason away from	to defend
		aphelion	from the sun	
cata	down	catechise	to sound down, or in the ear	to teach—to question
dia	through	diarrhœa	a flowing through	name of a disease
en or em	in	energy	inward power	force—spirit
		empiric	one skilled in practice alone	a quack, or pretender
epi or eph	on or upon	epitome	a cutting upon, as a book	an abridgment
		ephemeral	for a day	brief, or short
ec or ex	out	exegesis	a leading out	an explanation
hyper	beyond	hyperborean	beyond the north	cold, frigid
hypo	under	hypocrite	one under a mask	a feigner—dissembler
meta or meth	after	metaphysics	after physics	mental science
		method	after a way	order
para	side by side	parable	thrown side by side	a comparison
		paradigm	something shown side by side	a model, or example
		parasite	one near for food	a flatterer
peri	round	period	the way round	stated time, or end
		peripatetics	followers of Aristotle, who taught walking about	
syn, syl or sym	together, with	synod	a going together	an ecclesiastical assembly
		syllable	a taking together	a distinct utterance
		symphony	a sounding together	agreement

The prefixes, words and parts, have different shades of meaning.

AFFIXES.—(Sometimes called *postfixes* or *suffixes*.)

Affixes are letters or syllables placed at the end of a word to modify its meaning.

The affixes usually determine the part of speech to which the words they form belong, and therefore may be arranged according to the classes of words formed by their aid.

Some terminations have several meanings, and are used in forming different parts of speech—as, *ate*, in captiv*ate* and potent*ate*; *ish*, in burn*ish* and black*ish*; *en*, in weak*en* and wood*en*.

The same word is often used for the act and the product; the state and the quality; the place where and the practice of some art in it—as, formation, animate, surgery.

Affixes which form Nouns.

1. Affixes which denote the *person who acts, or who is.*

Anglo-Saxon—ar, and, er, yer, ster. *Classic*—an, ant, ary, ate, ee, eer, ent, ic, ist, ite, ive, or.

Examples.

Liar, one who tells lies.
Coward, one who is afraid.
Antiquary, one who studies old things.
Patentee, one to whom a patent is granted.
Oculist, one who professes to cure the eye.
Vagrant, one who wanders
Mountaineer, one who lives among the mountains.
Favorite, one who is favored.
Captive, one who is taken in war.
Gamester, one who gambles.

The pupil should be required to explain the following list of words, under each class, in a similiar manner:—

ar	beggar, bursar, scholar, vicar.
ard	dotard, drunkard, sluggard, steward, wizard.
er	brazier, butler, draper, mariner, talker, walker.
yer	lawyer, sawyer.
ster	barrister, chorister, maltster, punster, spinister.
an	Christian, European, Canadian, librarian, veteran.
ant	assailant, combatant, mendicant, lieutenant, litigant.
ary	contemporary, incendiary, lapidary, voluptuary.
ate	advocate, curate, delegate, legate, potentate.
ee	assignee, employee, legatee, referee, refugee.

eer — auctioneer, charioteer, mutineer, pioneer, scrutineer.
ent — adherent, client, patient, president, regent, student.
ic — critic, domestic, demoniac, mechanic, sceptic.
ist — botanist, linguist, monopolist, naturalist.
ite — [illegible], cosmopolite, eremite, Canaanite.
ive — fugitive, native, operative, representative.
or — ancestor, benefactor, competitor, malefactor.

4. Affixes which denote the *thing* which is, or is done.

Classic—ary, ice, ment, mony, ory.

Examples.

Boundary, that which bounds.
Testimony, that which is testified.
Aliment, that which nourishes.
Territory, the land which belongs to any one.

ary — anniversary, corollary, luminary, preliminary.
ice — advice, device, justice, notice, practice, service.
ment — advertisement, [illegible], amusement, document.
mony — alimony, patrimony, sanctimony.
ory — [illegible], directory, memory, promontory.

5. Affixes which denote the *place* where a thing is, or is done.

ry, ery, ary, ory.

Examples.

Vestry, a place where vestments are kept.
Aviary, a place where birds are kept.
Fishery, a place where fish are caught.
Armory, a place where arms are kept.

ry — [illegible], laundry, drapery.
ery — [illegible], [illegible], [illegible], [illegible], surgery.
ary — apiary, granary, dispensary, library.
ory — [illegible], factory, observatory, oratory.

6. Affixes which denote *rank*, *office*, or *dominion*.

Anglo-Saxon—dom, ric, ship. *Classic*—acy, ate.

Examples.

Dukedom, the rank of a duke.
Curacy, the office of a curate.
Bishopric, the jurisdiction of a bishop.
Kingdom, the dominion of a king.

dom & ric	Christendom, heathendom, earldom, archbishopric
ship	clerkship, mastership, professorship.
acy, cy	abbacy, captaincy, magistracy, papacy.
ate	electorate, protectorate, pontificate.

5. Affixes which denote *persons or things collectively.*

age, ry.

Examples.

Assemblage, a collection of persons.

Foliage, the leaves of a tree or forest.

Yeomanry, the farmers of a country.

age	coinage, cordage, leakage, plumage
ry	finery, gentry, machinery, peasantry.

6. Affixes which denote the *act of doing, or the thing done.*

age, ion, ment, ure.

Examples.

Pillage, the act of plundering, or theft.

Operation, the act of working, or the process.

Sepulture, the act of burying, or burial.

Entertainment, the act of treating guests, or a feast.

age	carriage, marriage, passage, postage.
ion	admission, dissection, inspection, passion.
ment	atonement, commencement, elopement, interment.
ure	creature, capture, disclosure, departure, imposture.

7. Affixes which denote *state, condition, quality.*

Anglo-Saxon—dom, hood, ness, ry, ship, th. *Classic*—acy, age, ance, ancy, ence, ency, ism, ment, mony, tude, ty or ity, ure.

Examples.

Widowhood, the state of being a widow.

Holiness, state of being holy.

Partnership, state of being a partner.

Activity, state of being active.

Vassalage, condition of a vassal.

Diligence, quality of being diligent.

dom — freedom, thraldom, martyrdom, wisdom.
hood — boyhood, girlhood, likelihood, priesthood, manhood.
ness — bitterness, deafness, darkness, gentleness, weakness.
ry — bravery, gallantry, pedantry, rivalry, slavery.
ship — apprenticeship, friendship, hardship, suretiship.
th — [illegible]th, truth, mirth, strength, youth.
acy — accuracy, degeneracy, legitimacy, supremacy.
age — bondage, dotage, marriage, peerage, pilgrimage.
ance, ancy — abundance, brilliancy, repentance, pliancy.
ence, ency — patience, effulgence, clemency, potency.
ism — barbarism, parallelism, schism, truism.
ment — agreement, banishment, enjoyment, punishment.
mony — acrimony, matrimony, parsimony.
tude — altitude, aptitude, gratitude, servitude, solitude.
ty or ity — brevity, captivity, ductility, felicity, poverty.
ure — composure, pleasure, rupture, torture, verdure.

8. Affixes which denote *art, science, practice, or doctrines.*

Anglo-Saxon—ry. *Classic*—ics, ism, ure.

Examples.

Cookery, the art of cooking.	Calvinism, the doctrines of Calvin
Optics, the science of seeing.	Sculpture, the art of carving.

ry — bribery, carpentry, chemistry, roguery, treachery.
ics — ethics, mathematics, physics, politics, tactics.
ism — criticism, [illegible], patriotism, [illegible], polytheism.
ure — agriculture, architecture, manufacture.

9. Affixes which denote *diminution* or *little*

Anglo-Saxon—el or le, kin, let or et, ling, ock, y or ie.
Classic—ule, cule or ule.

Examples.

Leaflet, a little leaf	Canticle, a little song.
Gosling, a little goose.	Reticule, a little net.
Paddock, a little park	Graticule, a little grate.

el, le — [illegible], kestrel, [illegible].
kin, en — lambkin, manikin, kitten, chicken.
let, et — [illegible], floweret, turret, eaglet, [illegible], rivulet.
ling — darling, duckling, foundling, stripling, seedling.

ock	bullock, hillock.
y or ie	Tommy, Willie, Jamie, lassie, baby.
cle, cule	conventicle, icicle, animalcule.
ule	globule, spherule.

Affixes which form Adjectives.

1. Affixes denoting *of, like, or pertaining to.*

ac, al, an, ar, ary, ic, ical, id, ile, ine, ory; ch, ese, ish.

Examples.

Dental, pertaining to the teeth.
Lunar, pertaining to the moon.
Angelic, pertaining to angels.
Lucid, pertaining to light.
Canine, pertaining to a dog.
Romish, pertaining to Rome.

ac	cardiac, elegiac, hypochondriac.
al	autumnal, final, paternal, royal, vernal.
an	cerulean, human, republican, sylvan, Canadian.
ar	circular, globular, lunar, ocular, singular.
ary	capillary, honorary, military, pecuniary.
ic	chaotic, despotic, domestic, gigantic, public.
ical	botanical, clerical, nautical, technical, poetical.
id	candid, fervid, humid, morbid, splendid.
ile	febrile, hostile, infantile, juvenile, mercantile.
ine	aquiline, feline, masculine, saline, divine.
ory	consolatory, piscatory, promissory, valedictory.
ch	Scotch, Welsh, French.
ese	Chinese, Genoese, Maltese, Portuguese.
ish	English, Irish, British, Danish, Swedish.

2. Affixes denoting *full of, or abounding in.*

Anglo-Saxon—ful, some, y. *Classic*—ous, ose, ate

Examples.

Faithful, full of faith.
Frolicsome, full of fun.
Knotty, full of knots.
Joyous, full of joy.
Jocose, full of jokes.
Passionate, full of passion.

ful	artful, careful, doleful, grateful, slothful.
some	burdensome, gladsome, humorsome, wholesome.
y	balmy, cloudy, flowery, mighty, massy, rocky.
ous	ambitious, beauteous, dubious, erroneous, timorous.

ose comatose, morbose, morose, verbose.
ate considerate, fortunate, moderate, ornate, intricate.

3. Affixes denoting *likeness*.

Anglo-Saxon—ish, like, ly; as—

Boyish, like a boy. Manlike, like a man. Friendly, like a friend.

ish brutish, clownish, knavish, foolish, monkish.
like Christianlike, giantlike, warlike, Godlike, ladylike.
ly brotherly, cowardly, matronly, princely, worldly.

4. Affixes denoting *may or can do, or be*.

Classic—able, ible, ile, ive

Examples.

Arable, can be ploughed. Ductile, can be drawn out.
Audible, may be heard. Active, able to act.

able blamable, curable, eatable, imitable, practicable.
ible flexible, legible, intelligible, tangible, visible.
ile docile, fragile, tractile, versatile.
ive cohesive, defensive, locomotive, productive.

5. Affixes denoting *being or doing*.

Classic—ant or ent; *like or made of*; *Anglo-Saxon*—en.

Examples.

Dormant, being asleep. Flaxen, like flax, or made of flax
Pendant, hanging down. Earthen, made of earth

ant errant, pleasant, verdant, vigilant.
ent [illegible], [illegible], belligerent, malevolent.
en brazen, golden, leaden, silken, woolen, wooden

6. Affixes denoting *diminution and privation*.

Anglo-Saxon—ish and less

Brackish, a little salt Saltless, without salt

ish darkish, feverish, greenish, [illegible], whitish.
less blameless, breathless, friendless, harmless, lifeless

The termination some denotes a degree of the quality indicated—as blithesome, delightsome, gladsome, lonesome, [illegible], wholesome.

The termination *th*, added to the cardinal numbers, forms the ordinal numbers, which are adjectives—as four, fourth; six, sixth.

The terminations *ern* and *erly*, and *ward*, added to north, east, south, and west, form adjectives expressing direction—as north, northern, northernly, northward.

Affixes which form Verbs.

Affixes which signify *to make, take, or give.*

Anglo-Saxon—en, ish. *Classic*—ate, fy, ise or ize.

Examples.

Brighten, to make bright.
Publish, to make public.
Apologize, to make an excuse.
Eradicate, to take the roots out.
Amplify, to make large.
Equalize, to make equal.

en cheapen, enlighten, gladden, moisten, quicken.
ish admonish, embellish, establish, impoverish, finish.
ate calculate, captivate decapitate, perforate, terminate.
fy fortify, magnify, qualify, rectify, sanctify, verify.
ise authorize, fertilize, pulverize, scrutinize.

Some verbs are formed by adding *l* or *le*, *r* or *er*—as hand, handle start, startle; knee, kneel; draw, drawl; wave, waver; long, linger; spit, sputter; whine, whimper.

Affixes which form Adverbs.

1. Affixes denoting *manner*—ly and wise.

Examples.

Artfully, in an artful manner.
Justly, in a just manner.
Honestly, in an honest manner.
Crosswise, in a cross manner.
Likewise, in a like manner.
Otherwise, in another manner.

2. Affixes denoting *direction*—ward.

Eastward, in the direction of the east; so westward, etc.
Heavenward, in the direction of heaven; so homeward, etc.
Leeward, in the direction opposite that from which the wind blows.
Thitherward, in the direction of that place—so whitherward.

The termination *ward* forms both adjectives and adverbs—as, he travelled north*ward*, in an awk*ward* manner, by the down*ward* road.

LATIN ROOTS.

acer (acris), sharp.—acrid, acridity, acrimony, acerbity: eager.
acidus, sour.—acid, acidity, acidulate.
acuo, I sharpen—acute,-ly,-ness, acumen.
aedes, a house—edifice, edif-y,-ication, unedifying.
aequus, equal—equalize, equality, equator, equation, equable; adequate equinox, equity, iniquity.
aestimo, I value—estimate, estimable, estimation; esteem
ager (agri), a field—acre, agrarian, peregrinate, pilgrim: agriculture,-al,-ist.
agger, a heap—exaggerate, exaggeration.
ago (actus), I do—act, actor, activity, actuate, exact, transact; agent, agitate, cogent, damage, manage, agile, agility; virago.
alienus, belonging to another—alien,-ate,-ated,-ation,-able.
alo, I nourish—aliment,-ated,-tion,-iveness.
alter, another—alter,-nate,-nation,-cation; subaltern.
altus, high—altitude, exalt, ation; altar.
amo (amicus), I love—amity, amicable, amiable, amorous, amatory, enamoured, inimical, enmity, enemy.
amplus, large—ample, ampli,-fy,-fication,-tude.
ango (anxi), I vex—anger, angry, anguish, anxiety, anxious,-ly.
angulus, a corner—angle, angular, rectangular, triangular, quadrangle.
anima, the soul or life—anim-al,-ate,-ation,-alcule; inanimate.
animus, the mind—unanimous, animosity, equanimity.
annus, a year—annual, biennial, perennial, millenium; annals, anniversary, annuity, annular, centenary.
antiquus, old or ancient—antique, antiquity, antiquated, antiquarian: antic.
aperio, I open—aperient, aperture; April.
appello, I call—appeal, appell-ative, ation.
apto, I fit—adapt, apt,-itude,-ly,-ness, adept, inept,-itude,-ly, ness.
aqua, water—aqueous, aquatic, aqueduct, terraqueous, aquarium.
arbiter, an umpire, a judge—arbiter, arbitr-ate,-ation, ary, ator, -ess
arbor, a tree—arbor, -eous, -escent, -etum, -ist
arceo, I shut up, restrain—coerce, coercive, coercion; exercise.
arcus, a bow—arc, arcade, arch, archer, archery.
ardeo, I burn—ardent, ardor, arduous, arson
arguo, I argue—arguer, argument, ation,-ative.
arma, arms—arm,-or,-orer, ory,-y,-ament,-orial,-istice; disarm, unarmed.

aro, I plough—arable, inarable, aration.
ars (*arti*), art—art,-ist,-isan,-ifice,-ificial,-ful, less; inert, inertness, inertia.
artus (*articulus*), a joint—article, articul ate,-ated,-ately, at on; inarticulate.
asper, rough—asperity, aspir ate,-ation; exasper-ate,-ation.
atrox, cruel—atrocity, atrocious,-ness.
audio, I hear—aud it,-tor,-itory,-ience,-ible; inaudible.
augeo (*auctus*), I increase—augment,-ation; auction,-eer; august,-tumn; author,-ity; auxiliary, unauthorized.
auris, the ear—aurist, auricle, auricular; auscultation.
avarus, greedy—avarice, avaricious,-ly,-ness.
avidus, eager—avidity.

barba, a beard—barb, barbed, barber, barbel.
barbarus, rude, savage—barbarian, barbar-ous,-ity, ize,-ism,-ic.
beatus, blessed—beatitude, beauty, beatific.
bellum, war—belligerent, rebel, rebellion.
bene, well (*used in composition*)—benefit, benevolent, benison, benifice, beneficent.
bibo, I drink—imbibe, bib, bibber, bibulous, bibacious; winebibber
bis (*bi*), twice—biped, bisect, biscuit, binary; combine.
bonus, good—boon, bounty, bounteous, bountiful.
brevis, short—brief, briefly, brevity, abbrevi-ate,-ation,-ator; breviary.
brutus, stupid—brutal,-ize,-ity; brutish,-ly,-ness; imbrute.

cado (*cas, cid*), I fall—cadence, case, casuist, casual, cascade; accident, accidence, coincide, coincidence, decay, deciduous, incident, occident, occasion.
caedo (*cid, cis*), I cut—caesura, concise, decide, decisive, decision, excision, incision, precise, precision; homicide, regicide, suicide, etc.
calculus, a little pebble—calculate, calcul,-able,-ation,-ator; miscalculate, incalculable.
candeo, I am white, I shine—candid, candidate, candor, candle; incense, incentive.
cano (*cant*), I sing—cant, canticle, chant, enchant, incantation, recant, accent.
capillus, a hair—capillary, capillarity, capilliform

capio (cap, capt), I take—capable,-acious,-acity, accept; captious,-ive,-ivate,-or, -ure; except, precept, intercept; [illegible], [illegible], [illegible], receipt, [illegible], acceptation, occupation, preceptor, receptacle, susceptibility.

caput (capitis), the head—capital, capitulate, cape, captain, chapter, precipitate, precipice, recapitulate.

caro (carnis), flesh—incarnate, carnal, carnage, carnival, carrion, [illegible], carnivorous.

causa, a cause—causation, accuse, excuse, recusant.

caveo (cautum), to be on one's guard—caution, cautious,-ly,-ness, precaution.

cavus, hollow—cave, cavern, concave, cavity, excavate.

cedo (cess), I yield, I go—cede, cession, cease, cessation, accede, concede, exceed, precede, proceed, recede, succeed, [illegible], [illegible], ive,-ion, etc.

celer, swift—celerity, accelerate.

celeber, renowned—celebrate,-ated,-ation, celebrity.

celsus, high—excel, excellent, excellence, excelsior.

censeo, I judge, I blame—censor, censorious, censure, censurable.

centrum, the centre—central, centrical; centripetal, centrifugal, concentrate, concentric; eccentric.

centum, a hundred—century, centurion; centage, centesimal, centipede.

cerno (cret), I judge—certain, certify, concern, decree, discern, discreet, [illegible], [illegible], secretary.

circus, a circle—circlet, circular, circulate, circuit, encircle, semicircle.

cito, I call or rouse—cite, citation, excite,-ment, incite, recite, recitation, [illegible].

civis, a citizen—civic, city, civil,-ian, ity, [illegible], uncivil.

clamo, I cry out—claim, acclaim, clamor, clamorous, declamation, exclaim, proclaim, proclamation, reclaim.

clarus, clear, bright—clear, [illegible], clarify, declare, declaration.

claudo (claus-clus) I close—close, closet, cloister, conclude, [illegible], [illegible], [illegible], [illegible], [illegible]

clemens, merciful, mild—clement, clemency, inclement, inclemency.

clino, I bend—decline, declension, declivity, incline, inclination, acclivity, recline.

colo (cult), I cultivate—cultivated, colony, colonist, colonial, colonise, culture, agriculture, uncult

colo, I strain—[illegible], colation, percolate, percolation.

communis, common—[illegible], community, [illegible].

cor (cordis), the heart—core, cordial, courage; concord, [illegible], discord, record, accord, [illegible].

cornu, a horn—corn, cornet, corneous, cornice, unicorn.
corona, a crown—crown, coronation, corolla, cornet, coroner
corpus (*corpor*), the body—corporal, corporate, corporation, corporeal, corpulent, corpse, corpuscle, incorporate.
credo, I trust, I believe—creed, credit, credible, creditor, credential, credulous, incredulity, accredit.
creo, I make—create, creator, creation, creature, creative, recreation.
cresco (*cret*), I grow—crescent, accretion, concretion, excrescence, decrease, increase, increment.
crimen, a crime—criminal, crimination, recrimin-ate,-ation.
crudus, raw, unripe—crude, crudity, crudeness.
crux (*cruc*), a cross—crucify, crucifixion, cruciform, crucible, crusade, excruciate, croiser, cross.
cubo, or **cumbo**, I lie down—cumber, cumbent, cumbrance, incubus, accumbent, incumbent, recumbent, succumb.
culpa, a fault—culpable, culpability, culprit, inculpate, exculpate.
cumulus, a heap—cumulative, accumul-ate,-ation,-ator.
cura, care—cure, curate, curacy, curious, accurate, secure, sinecure
curro (*curs*), I run—current, curricle, courier, concur, incur, occur, recur, succor, course, concurrence, discourse, incursion, precursor.
curvus, crooked—curve, curvature, curvate, incurvate.

damno, I condemn—damage, condemnable, condemnation, indemnify.
debeo, I owe—debit, debt, debtor, debenture, indebtedness.
decet, it is becoming—decent, decency, decorate, decoration, decorous, indecorous.
deleo, I blot out, I destroy—delete, indelible, deleterious,-ly,-ness.
deliciae, delight—delicacy, delicate,-ly,-ness, delicious.
dens (*dent*), a tooth—dental, dentist, dentifrice, dentition, indent, indenture, trident.
densus, thick—dense, density, condense, condensation.
deus, a god—deify, deity, deist, deism, deification.
dico (*dicat*), I set apart—dedicate, dedicatory, abdicate, index, indicate, indicative, predicate, predicament, adjudicate.
dexter, right-handed—dexter, dexterity, dexterous,-ly,-ness.
dico (*dict*), I say—diction, dictate, dictator, dictatorial, addict, benediction, contradiction, edict, interdict, valedictory, verdict.
dies, a day—dial, diary, diurnal, meridian, quotidian, diet.
dignus, worthy—dignify, dignity, indignity, deign, disdain, indignant, indignation, condign.
disco, I learn—disciple, discipline, disciplinary, disciplinarian.
divido,—I separate—divide, division, dividend, indivisible, individual.

divinus, heavenly—divine, divinity, divination.
do (dat. dit.) I give—donor, donation, date, dative, antedate, addition, condition, edit, editor, perdition, tradition, pardon.
doceo (doct), I teach—doctor, doctrine, document, docile, docility.
dominus, a master, a lord—dominant, dominion, domination, dominical, domineer, predominate.
domus, a house—dome, domestic, domesticate, domicile, domiciliary.
dubium, doubtful—dubious, dubitation, indubitable, doubt, doubtful.
duco (duct) I lead—duke, ducat, ductile, abduction, adduce, conduce, conduit, conduct, deduction, educate, inducement, reduce, seduce, traduce, aqueduct, viaduct.
durus, hard—endure, durable, duration, during, indurated, obdurate, obduracy.

ebrius, drunken—inebriate, inebriety, inebriation (with *sine*) sober, -ly, sobriety.
egeo, I am in need—indigent, indigence.
ego, I—egoism, egoist, egotize, egotistic, egotism.
elegans, handsome—elegant, elegance, inelegant.
emo (empt), I buy—exempt, exemption, pre-emption, peremptory, redeem, redemption; prompt, impromptu.
eo (it), I go—circuit, exit, initiate, iterate, obituary, perish, transit, transition.
equus, a horse—equine, equip, equipage, equipment.
erro, I wander—err, errant, error, errand, erratic, erroneous, aberration, errata.
esse (ess), to be—essence, essential, interest, nonentity, absent, present, represent, misrepresent.
exemplum, a model—example, exemplary, exemplify, unexampled, sample.
experior (expert), I try—experiment, experimental, expert, expertness, experience, peril.
exter, externus, outward—external, extraneous, extreme, extrinsic

faex (fæc), sediment, dregs—feces, feculence; defecate, defecation.
faber, a workman—fabric, fabricate, fabricator, fabrication
facies, the face—facial, efface, superficies, superficial
facilis, easy—facile, facility, facilitate, difficult, difficulty.
facio (fac, fect), I make—fact, faction, factory, fortify, affect, affectation, artifice, confection, defect, effectual, manufacture, efficacious, perfect, proficient, refection, sacrifice, sufficient.

fallo (*fals*), I deceive—false, falsity, fallacy, fallible, infallible, fault
falx, a hook or sickle—falcated, defalcate, defalcation.
fama, a report—fame, famous, infamous, defame, defamation.
familia, a family—familiar,-ity,-ize, unfamiliar.
fanum, a temple—fane, profane, profanity, fanatic, fanaticism.
fari (*fan, fat*), to speak—fate, fatal, fable, affable, ineffable, infant, nefarious, preface.
fateo (*fess*), I acknowledge—confess, confession, professional.
fatigo, I weary—fatigue, indefatigable, fag.
fatuus, silly—fatuous, fatuity, infatuated, infatuation.
fecundus, fruitful—fecund, fecundate, fecundity.
felix, happy—felicity, felicitous, infelicity, felicitate.
fendo (*fens*), I strike or ward off—fender, defend, defendant, offend, inoffensive; fence, defence.
fero (*lat*), I bear or carry—ferry, fertile, confer, defer, differ, infer, offering, preference, suffer, transference, collation, elate, odoriferous, prelate, superlative, translation.
ferrum, iron—ferreous, ferruginous, ferrule, farrier, farriery.
ferveo, I boil or rage—fervor, fervent, fervid, effervesce; fermentation, fever, feverish, febrifuge.
festus, joyful—festal, festive, festivity, festival, infect, fête.
fibra, a thread—fibre, fibril, fibrous, fibrine.
fido, I trust—fidelity, confide, defy, diffidence, infidelity, perfidious, perfidy.
figo (*fix*), I fasten—fix, fixture, affix, prefix, transfix, crucifix.
filius, a son; **filia**, a daughter—filial, affiliate, affiliation.
filum, a thread—file, filament, filigree, fillet, defile, profile.
fingo (*fict*), I form—fiction, fictitious, figment, effigy, figure, figurative, transfiguration.
finis, an end—finish, infinite, infinity, affinity, definite, indefinite.
firmus, strong—firm, firmament, affirm, confirm, infirm, infirmary, infirmity.
fiscus, a money-bag, the public treasury—fiscal, confiscate, confiscation.
fissum, a cleft—fissure, fissile, fission.
flamma, a flame—flambeau, inflame, inflammation, inflammatory.
flecto (*flex*), I bind—flector, flexion, flexible, deflect, inflection, reflection, reflex.
fligo (*flict*), I beat—afflict, affliction, conflict, infliction, profligate, profligacy.
flo (*flat*), I blow—flatulent, afflatus, efflation, inflate, inflation, flute.
flos, a flower—floral, florid, floridity, flour, flourish, flowery, efflorescence.
fluo (*fluct, flux*), I flow—fluid, fluent, fluvial, fluctuate, affluence, conflux, confluence, defluxion, effluvia, influence, superfluity.

fodio (fossum) I dig—fossilize, fossilist, fossiliferous.
foedus, a treaty—federal, confederate, confederacy.
folium, a leaf—foliage, foliaceous, foliate, foil, trefoil, folio.
forma, form, shape—formal, form,-ation,-ative,-ality,-ula, conformity, deformity, uniform, information, performance, reform, transformation, uniformity.
fors (fort), chance—fortune, fortunate, fortuitous, misfortune, unfortunate.
fortis, strong, brave—fortify, fortitude, force, enforce, fortress, effort, comfort.
frango (fract), I break—frangible, fraction, fracture, fragile, fragility, frailty, infringe, refraction, suffrage, irrefragable.
frater, a brother—fratern-al,-ity,-ize, fratricide; friar.
fraus, deceit—fraud, fraudulent; defraud.
frigus, cold—frigid, frigidity, frigorific, refriger-ate,-ator.
frons (front), the forehead—frontier, affront, confront, effrontery, front, frontlet, frontispiece.
fruor (fruct), I enjoy—frugal, frugality, fruit,-ful,-less,-lessness, fruition, fruiterer, fructify.
fugio, I flee—fugitive, fugacious, refuge, subterfuge.
fulgeo, I shine—fulgent, refulgent, effulgence, fulminate.
fumus, smoke—fume, fumigat-e,-ation,-ator, perfume.
fundo (fus), I pour out—fuse, fusible, a founder, confound, diffuse, effusion, profusion, suffusion, transfuse.
fundus, field, bottom—found, to founder, foundation, fundamental, profundity; fund, funds, refund.
fungor (funct), I perform—function, functional, functionary, perfunctory, defunct.

gelu, frost—gelid, gelatine, congeal, jelly.
gero (gest), I carry—gesture, gesticulate, belligerent, congestion, digest, indigestion, register, suggest, vicegerent, jest, or
gigno (gen), I bring forth or produce—generate, generation, genealogical, generic, general, genitive, generous, generosity, genuine, gentile, gentry, genial, indigenous, ingenuous, ingenuity, progenitor, progeny, regenerate.
globus, a ball—globe, globular, globulous, conglobulate.
glacies, ice—glacier, glacial, glaciate.
gluten, glue—glue, glutinous, agglutinate, conglutinate.
gradior (gress), I go—grade, gradation, gradual, graduate, degrade, retrograde; ingress, progress, transgression, congress.
gramen, grass—graminivorous, gramineous, [illegible]

grandis, great—grand, grandeur, grandee, grandsire, aggrandize, grandiloquent, grandiose.

granum, a grain of corn—granary, garner, granule, granulate, grange, granate, grenade, grenadier.

gratus, thankful—grateful, gratitude, gratuity, gratify, congratulate, grace, gracious, disgrace, greet, ingratiate, ingratitude.

gravis, heavy—grave, gravity, gravitate, grief, grieve, grevious, aggrieve, aggravate.

grex (*greg*), a flock—gregarious, congregate, aggregate, egregious, segregate.

gusto, I taste—gust, disgust, disgustful, disgustingly.

habeo (*hib*), I have—habitation, habit,-ual, cohabit, debilitate; exhibit, inhibit, prohibition.

haereo (*hes*), I stick—adhere, adhesive, cohesion, coherent, hesitate, inherent, incoherent.

haeres (*haered*), an heir—heritage, heritable, hereditary, inherit,-ance, disinherit; heiress, heirloom, co-heir.

halo, I breathe—exhale, inhale, inhalation, anhelation.

haurio (*haust*), I draw—exhaust,-ible,-ion,-less,-ive; inexhaustible

herba, an herb—herbage, herbalist, herbaceous, herbivorous.

hilaris, cheerful—hilarity, hilarious, exhilaration.

homo, a man—human, humane, homage, humanity, humanize, homicide, inhumanity.

horreo, I shudder—horror, horrid, horrible, horrify, abhor, abhorrence.

hortor, I advise—exhort, exhortation, hortative, hortatory, dehortatory.

hospes (*hospit*), a guest—hospitable, hospital,-ity, host, hotel, hostler.

hostis, an enemy—host, hostile, hostility, hostage.

humeo, I am moist—humid, humidity, humor, humorist, humorous.

humus, the ground—inhume, exhume, exhumation, posthumous, humble, humility.

idem, the same—identity, identical, identify, identifiable.

ignis, fire—igneous, ignite, ignition, ignitible.

imago, an image—imagine, imaginary, imagination.

impero, I command—imperative, emperor, imperial.

impetus, force—impetus, impetuous,-ly,-ness, impetuosity.

inanis, empty—inane, inanity, inanition.

inferus, below—inferior, inferiority, infernal.

insula, an island—insulated, isle, isolate, peninsula.

integer, whole—integral, integrity, disintegrate, redintegration.

ira, anger—ire, ireful, irate, irascible, irritation.

jaceo, I lie—jacent, adjacent, circumjacent.
jacio (jact), I throw—jet, jaculation, ejaculate, abject, conjecture, dejection, interjection, objective, reject, subject, subjection.
jocus, a jest—joke, jocose, jocund, jocular, jocularity.
jubilo, I shout for joy—jubilee, jubilate, jubilation.
jugum, a yoke—abjugate, subjugate, subjugation.
jungo (junct), I join—junction, juncture, conjunction, conjugal, injunction; join, enjoin, joiner.
juro, I swear—jury, adjure, conjure, perjury.
judex, a judge; jus (jur), right—just, justice, justify, injury, judge, judicature, judicious, prejudice, judicial, jurisprudence.
juvenis, young—juvenile, juvenility, juniors, juniority, rejuvenescence.
juvo (jut), I help—adjutant, coadjutor.

labor, work—labor, laborious, laboratory, elaborate.
labor (laps), I slide—lapse, relapse, elapse, illapse, collapse.
laedo (lis, lid), I hurt—collide, collision, elide, elision.
lapis (lapid), a stone—lapidary, dilapidate, dilapidation.
latus, carried, broad—dilate, latitude, latitudinarian, delay, dilatory, illative, oblate, translation.
latus (later), a side—lateral, collateral, equilateral.
laus (laud), praise—laud, laudable, applaud, allow, allowable.
laxus, loose—lax, laxity, relax, relaxation, prolix.
lego (legat), I send, appoint—legate, legacy, delegate, allegation.
lego (lect), I read or choose—legible, lecture, legion, allege, college, diligent, eligible, elegant, election, negligence, selection.
legumen, pulse, pease, beans—leguminous, legume.
levis, light (levo, to raise)—levity, levy, alleviate, elevate, elevator; relieve.
lex (leg), a law—legal, legality, legalize, legislator, legitimate, allegiance.
liber, free—liberal, liberty, liberate, illiberal, livery.
liber, a book—library, librarian, libel, libellous.
libra, a balance—deliberate-ly,-ive, equilibrium, indeliberate.
licet, it is lawful—license, licentiate, licentious, illicit.
lignum, wood—ligneous, lignity, ligniform.
ligo, I bind—liable, liability, ligament, league, liege, alliance, oblige, religion.
limes, a boundary—limit, limited, illimitable, unlimited
linquo (lict), I leave—delinquent, dereliction, relinquish, relict, relic
linum, flax—linen, linsey, lint, line, lineal, delineate, lineament

liqueo, I melt—liquid, liquefy, liquefaction, liquidity, liquor.
litera, a letter—literal, literature, alliteration, illiterate, obliterate, letter.
locus, a place—local, locality, locate, locomotive, dislocate, allocation.
longus, long—longitude, longevity, elongate, prolong.
loquor, I speak—loquacity, soliloquy, eloquence, elocution, obloquy, magniloquent, ventriloquist.
ludo (*lus*), I play—ludicrous, allusion, elude, illusion, delusion, delusory, prelude.
lumen, light—luminary, illuminate, illumination, luminous.
luna, the moon—lunar, lunation, lunacy, lunatic, sublunary.
luo, I wash—ablution, alluvial, deluge, dilution, pollute.
lustro, I shine—lustration, illustrious, illustrate.
lux (*luc*), light—lucid, lucifer, elucidate, pellucid.
luxus, luxury, excess—luxuriant, luxurious,-ly,-ness.

macies, leanness—emaciate, emaciation.
magnus (*major*), great — magnify, magnitude, magistrate, master, major, majority, majestic; mayor.
malus, bad—malice, malicious, malevolent, malignity.

malleus, a hammer—mallet, malleable, maul, unmalleable
mando, I enjoin—mandate, command, demand, remand
maneo (*mans*), I remain—manse, mansion, immanent, permanent, remnant.
manus, the hand—manual, manufacture, manumission, manacles manuscript, emancipate.
mare, the sea—marine, mariner, maritime, submarine, mermaid
mater, mother—maternal, maternity, matron, matrimony, matriculate, matricide.
maturus, ripe—mature, maturity, immature, premature.
medeor, I heal—medical, medicine, remedy, irremediable.
medius, the middle—mediate, medium, immediate, mediocrity.
mel, honey—mellifluous, melliferous, mellitic.
memini, I remember; **memor**, mindful—memory, memorial, memorandum, memoir, commemorate, reminiscence.
mens, the mind—mental, mentality, demented, amentia.
mergo (*mers*), I plunge—mersion, emerge, emergency, immersion, submerse.
merx, merchandise—commerce, commercial, merchant, mercantile
metior (*mens*), I measure—mete, immense, mensuration, dimension, commensurate.

migro, I remove—migrate, emigrate, immigration, transmigration.
miles, a soldier—militia, military, militant, militate.
mineo, I project—imminent, prominent, eminent, eminence.
minister, a servant—ministration, ministry, adminis-ter,-trate,-trator.
minor (minus), less—diminish, diminution, comminution, minority, minute.
mirus, wonderful—miracle, admire, admiration, admirable.
misceo (mixtus), I mingle—mixture, miscellaneous, unmixed, promiscuous, intermix.
miser, wretched—miser, miserable, misery, commiserate.
mitto (missus), I send—mission, missile, admit, commission, dismiss, missionary, manumission, promise, remission.
modus, a manner—moderate, accommodate, commodious, mode, model, modify, modulate, modest.
mons, a mountain—mount, mound, amount, dismount, paramount, tantamount.
mollis, soft—mollify, mollient, emollient.
moneo, I advise—monitor, monument, admonish, premonition.
monstro, I show—monstrous, demonstrate, demonstrable, remonstrate.
mordeo, I bite—mordant, morsel, remorse, remorseless.
mors (mortis), death—mortal, mortality, immortal, -ize, mortify.
mos (moris), a custom—moral, moralize, morality, immoral, demoralize.
moveo (motus), I move—remove, commotion, promotion, remote.
multus, many—multitude, multiple, multiplication, multiplied.
munus, a gift, or office—munificence, commun-ion, -icate, immunity, remunerative.
murus, a wall—mural, immure.
musa, a song—muse, music, amuse, amusement, museum.
muto, I change—mutable, mutation, mutual, permutation, transmute.

narro, I relate—narration, narrative, narrator.
nascor (natus), to be born—nascent, native, nation, nature, innate, supernatural.
navis, a ship—navy, naval, navig-ate,-ation,-able.
necto (nexus), I tie—connect, annex, annexation, disconnect.
nervus, a sinew—nervous, unnerve, enervate.
neuter, neither of the two—neutral,-ize,-ity.
nihil, nothing—[illegible], nihility, annihilate,-ation.
nobilis, well-known—noble, nobility, [illegible], ignoble.
noceo, I hurt—[illegible], [illegible], [illegible], [illegible], [illegible].
nomen, a name—nominal, nominate, denomination, [illegible], nomenclature, ignominy.

norma, a rule—normal, abnormal, enormous, enormity.
nosco, cognosco, I know—cognizance, recognition, knowledge, acknowledge, recognize, precognition.
notus, known—note, notable, notorious, annotator.
novus, new—novel, novelty, novitiate, innovate, renovate.
nox (*noct*), night—equinox, equinoctial, nocturnal.
nullus, none—nullify, nullity, annual, disannul.
numerus, a number—numerous, numeration, enumerate, innumerable, supernumerary.
nuncio, I tell—announce, enunciate, denounce, renounce, pronunciation.
nutrio, I nourish—nutriment, nutrition, nutritive, innutritious.

obscurus, dark—obscur-e,-ation, obscurely, obscureness, obscurity.
oculus, the eye—ocular, oculist, binocular, inoculate.
odor, smell—odorous, odoriferous, odorless.
oleo, I smell—olfactory, redolent, redolence.
olo or **olesco**, I grow—adolescence, adult, abolish, abolition, abolitionist.
omnis, all—omnipotent, omniscience, omnivorous, omnibus.
onus (*oner*), a burden—onerous, onerary, exoner-ate,-ation,-ative.
opus (*oper*), a work—oper-ate,-ative,-ation,-ator, co-operate, opera.
orbis, a globe—orb, orbit, orbicular, exorbitant.
ordo, law—order, disorder, extraordinary, ordain, ordination, subordinate.
opto, I wish—option, optional, optative, adopt, adoption.
orior, I rise—orient, origin, originate, exordium.
orno, I deck—ornament,-al,-ation, adorn, adornment, ornate.
oro, I speak—oracle, oration, oral, oratary, orator, orison, adore, inexorable, peroration.
os (*ossis*), a bone—osseous, ossify, ossific, ossivorous.
ovum, an egg—oval, ovate, ovally, oviparous.

pallium, a cloak, covering—palliate, palliative, palliation.
pando, I spread—expand, expansive, expanse, pace, space, compass, surpass, trespass.
pango (*pact*), I fix or agree—paction, compact, compactness, impinge.
palatum, the roof of the mouth, taste—palate, palatal, palatable, unpalatable.
palus, a peg or post—pale, paling, palisade, empale, empalement.
par, equal—parity, separate, disparity, disparage, peer, peerless.

pareo, I appear—peer, appear, apparition, apparent, transparent.

pario, I bring forth—parent, parental, oviparous, viviparous.

paro, I make ready—preparation, pare, parade, parry, apparel, prepare, repair, reparation.

pars, a part—particle, partake, partition, party, partisan, partial, partner, parboil, parcel, apartment, impart, impartiality.

pasco (*past*), I feed—pastor, pastoral, pasture, antepast, repast.

pater, a father—paternal, paternity, patrimony, patron, patronize, patrician.

patior (*pass*), I suffer—patience, patient, impatient, passive, passionate, compassion.

patria, one's country—patriot, patriotism, compatriot, expatriate.

pax, peace—peace, pacify, pacific, pacification.

pello (*puls*), I drive—pulse, pulsation, compel, dispel, expulsion, impulse, repulsion.

pello, I name or call—appellative, compellation, appeal, repeal.

pendeo, I hang—pendant, pendulum, depend, impend, suspense, appendix.

pendo (*pens*), I weigh—pensive, expensive, expenditure, compensation, dispense, recompense, stipend, stipendiary.

penetro, I pierce—penetrate, penetration, impenetrable.

pes (*ped*), the foot—pedal, pedestal, pedestrian, biped, quadruped, expedite, expedient, impediment.

peto, I seek—petition, petulant, appetite, compete, competitor, impetus, impetuous, repeat, repetition.

pingo (*pict*), I paint—picture, pigment, pictorial, picturesque, depict.

pius, dutiful—piety, impious, impiety.

placeo, I please—placid, complacency, complaisant, displease, implacable.

planta, a plant—plantation, plantain, implant, supplant, transplant.

plaudo (*plaus*), I praise—plaudit, applaud, plausible, applause, explode, explosion.

pleo (*plet*), I fill—plenary, plenty, complement, complete, depletion, replenish, supply, supplement.

plico, I fold—apply, complicate, complex, display, duplicity, explicate, implicit, perplex, simple, triplet.

ploro, I wail—deplore, explore, implore.

pluma, a feather—plumage, plume, plumeless, plumule.

poena, pain or punishment—pain, penal, penalty, penance, penitentiary, impunity, repent.

polio, I smooth—polish, polite, interpolation.

pondus (*ponder*), weight—pound, ponderous, ponder, preponderate, imponderable

pono (*posit*), I place—post, posture, position, apposite, apposition, deposition, dispose, expositor, propose, purpose, repose, transposition.
populus, the people—popular, populace, population, depopulate, public, publish, republic.
porto, I carry—porter, portable, export, import, importunity, report, transportation.
potens, powerful—potent, potentate, potential,-ity,-ly, impotent, omnipotent.
poto, I drink—potation, potion, potable.
praeda, plunder—prey, predatory, predaceous, depred-ation,-ator
prehendo, I take—apprehend, comprehension, apprentice, reprehend
premo (*press*), I press—print, pressure, compress, depression, express, oppression, repress, suppression, irrepressible.
pretium, a price—precious, appreciate, prize appraise, depreciation
primus, first—prime, primate, primer, prince, principal, primogeniture.
privo, I take away—deprive, privation, privative.
privus, one's own or single—private, privacy, privilige.
probo, I prove—probe, probation, probable, approbation, improve, disprove, reprobate.
promo (*prompt*), I bring forth, I tell—prompter, prompt, promptly, promptitude, impromptu.
probe (*prox*), near—propinquity, propitiate, proximate, approximate, approach.
proprius, one's own—proper, property, appropriate, propriety, impropriety.
pudor, shame—impudent, impudence, repudiate.
pugno, I fight—pugnacious, pugilist, impugn, repugnance.
pulmo, the lungs—pulmonary, pulmonic.
pulvis (*pulver*), dust—pulverize, pulverable, pulverization.
pungo (*punct*), I prick—pungent, puncture, punctuation, punctilli-us, punctuality, compunction, expunge, point, appoint.
purgo, I cleanse—purge, purgative, purgatory, purgatorial.
purus, clean—purify, purity, puritan, impure, impurity.
pus (*pur*) matter of a sore—pustule, pustulate, purulent, suppurate.
puto, I reckon, I prune—putative, compute, dispute, deputy, imputation, repute; amputate.
putris, rotten—putrefy, putrefaction, putrid, putridity, putrescence

qualis, of what kind—qualify, quality, disqualify.
quantum, how much—quantity, quantitative.
quaero (*quis*, *ques*), I seek—quest, question, acquire, disquisition, inquire, request, requisition, perquisite.

quatio, I shake—quash, concussion, discuss, percussion.
quatuor, four—quart, quarter, quartern, quadruped, quadrant.
quies, rest—quiet, quiescence, inquietude, disquietude, acquiesce.
quot, how many—quote, quotient, quotation, quotidian.

radius, a ray—radiant, radiation, irradiate, radius.
radix, a root—radicle, radical, radish, eradicate.
rado (rasum), I scrape—raze, razor, erase, abrasion, rasure.
ramus, a branch—ramify, ramification.
rapio, I carry off—rapacious, rapid, rapine, rapture, surreptitious.
rarus, thin—rarefy, rarefaction, rare.
rego (rectum), I rule—regal, regent, regimen, regular, register, rector, reign, direct, rectify.
repo, I creep—reptile, reptilian.
res, a thing—real, realize, republic.
rideo (risum), I laugh—ridicule, ridiculous, risible, deride, derision.
rigeo, I am stiff—rigidity, rigor, rigorously.
rivus, a stream—river, rivulet, rival, rivalry, arrive, derive, derivation.
rodo (rosum), I gnaw—corrode, corrosion, corrosive, erosion.
rota, a wheel—rote, rotate, rotary; rotund, routine.
rudis, rude, ignorant—rudiment, erudite, erudition.
rus (ruris), the country—rural, rustic, rusticity, rusticate.
rumpo (ruptum), I break—rupture, abrupt, bankrupt, corruption, interrupt, irruption.

[illegible], [illegible]—[illegible], sacrifice, consecrate, execrable, sacrilege
[illegible], [illegible]—[illegible], [illegible], sagacity, presage.
sal, [illegible]—[illegible], saltish, [illegible], saucy.
salio (saltum), I leap—[illegible], [illegible], assault, sally, [illegible], exultation, insult, result, resilient.
salus (salutis), health—[illegible], [illegible], salubrious, salvage, salve, salvation.
[illegible], I [illegible]—sanction, sanctify, sanctity, saint, sanctuary.
sanguis (sanguinis), blood—[illegible], sanguinary, [illegible], [illegible].
sapio, taste, I am wise—sapient, savor, insipid, [illegible], insipidity.
satis, enough—satisfy, satisfaction, sate, satiate, insatiable.
scando, I climb—[illegible], [illegible], [illegible], [illegible], [illegible].
[illegible], I cut—[illegible], scissors, [illegible], rescind, [illegible]

scio, I know—science, scientific, sciolist, conscience, omniscience, prescience.

scribo (*script*), I write—scribe, scripture, scribble, description, inscribe, manuscript, superscription.

sculpo, I carve—sculptor, sculpture, sculptured.

seco (*sect*), I cut—sect, section, dissect, insect, intersection, trisect.

sedeo (*sess*), I sit—seat, sedate, sedentary, session, assiduous, preside, possess, supersede.

semen, seed—seminal, seminary, disseminate.

senex, old—senile, senator, senior, seniority, seignior.

sentio (*sens*), I feel, I think—sense, sensuous, sensitive, sensible, sentient, sentiment, sentence, assent, dissension.

sequor (*secut*), I follow—second, sequence, execute, subsequent, prosecute, obsequies, subsequent.

sero (*sert*), I knit or join—series, assert, insertion, desertion, exert

serpo, I creep—serpent, serpentine, serpentize.

servo, I keep or wait—serve, servant, servile, servitude, conserve, observe, preservation, subservience.

severus, strict—severe, severity, persevere, asseveration.

signum, a mark—sign, signify, assign, consignment, designate, resignation, insignificant.

silex, flint—silicious, silicate, silicify.

similis, like—similar, similarity, similitude, assimilate, resemble, dissimulation, simulation.

sinus, a curve or bay—insinuate, sinuosity.

socius, a companion—social, sociable, society, association, dissociate.

sol, the sun—solar, parasol, solarize.

solidus, solid—solidity, solidify, solder, consolidate.

solvo, I loose—solvency, solve, solution, soluble, absolve, absolute, revolution.

solus, alone—sole, solitude, solitary, desolate, soliloquy.

sono, I sound—sonnet, sonorous, consonant, dissonance, resound, unison.

sorbeo, I suck in—absorbent, absorb,-ing, absorption, reabsorb.

sors (*sort*), a lot—sort, assort, consort, resort, sorcery.

spargo (*spers*), I scatter—asperse, aspersion, disperse, intersperse.

spatium, space—spacious, expatiate, spaciousness.

specio, **specto**, I look—special, specious, specimen, spectacle, spectator, aspect, conspicuous, expect, prospect, suspicion.

spero, I hope—desperate, despair, prosper, prosperity.

spiro, I breathe—spirit spiritual, sprite, aspirant, conspire, dispirit, expiration, uninspired.

splendeo, I shine—splendid, splendor, resplendent.

spondeo (sponsum), I promise—sponsor, spouse, correspondence, irresponsible, respond.
sponte, of one's own will—spontaneous, -ly, -ness, spontaneity.
statuo, I set up, I appoint—statue, statute, constitute, institute, institution, substitute.
stella, a star—stellar, constellation, stellated, stellular.
stilla, a drop—still, distil, instil, distillation.
stinguo (stinctum), I put out—distinguish, distinct, extinguish, extinct, instinctive.
sto (stare, stati), I stand—stable, establish, state, station, stationary, constant, distant, instantaneous, obstacle, rest, solstice, substantive, substitute.
stratum, thrown down—strata, prostrate, stratify, stratification.
stringo (strictum), I bind fast—stringent, astringent, strict, stricture, strain, constrain, restrict, restrain, distrain, distress, unrestrained.
struo (structum), I build—destroy, destructive, instruct, instrument, superstructure.
stupeo, I am stunned, amazed—stupid, -ly, -ity, stupendous.
sumo (sumptum), I take—assume, consumption, presume, resume, sumptuary, sumptuous.
surgo (surrectum), I rise—insurgent, insurrection, resurrection.

tango (tactum), I touch—tangent, tangible, tactility, contact, contagion, contagious, contingent.
tego (tectum), I cover—tegument, protect, detection, protectorate.
temno (temptum), I despise—contemn, contemptible, contemptuous.
tempus, time—temporal, contemporary, extemporaneous.
tendo (tensum), I stretch—tendency, attend, extension, intention, ostentation, pretence, subtend.
teneo (tentum), I hold—tenable, tenant, tenet, contain, detention, abstinence, continence, impertinent, sustain, obtain, entertainment.
tenuis, thin—tenuity, attenuate, extenuate.
terminus, a bound—term, terminate, determine, exterminate, interminable.
tero (tritum), I rub—trite, triturate, trit, attrition, contrition, detriment.
terra, the earth—terrestrial, terraqueous, terrace, inter, subterraneous.
terreo, I frighten—terrible, deter, deterrent, terror.
testis, a witness—test, testify, testament, attest, detest, intestate, protestation.
texo, I weave—textile, texture, context, pretext, tissue.
timeo, I fear—timorous, timidity, timid.

tolero, I bear—tolerant, tolerable, intolerant, toleration.

torpeo, I am benumbed—torpid, torpidity, torpidly.

torqueo (*tort*), I twist—torture, tortuous, torment, contortion, distort, extortion, retort.

torreo, I parch—torrid, toast, torrefy, torrent.

totus, the whole—total, totality, totally.

traho (*tract*), I draw—trace, tractable, tractile, attract, abstract, distraction, extraction, portray, retract, protract.

tremo, I shake, tremble—tremendous, tremble, tremulous.

trepidus, fearful—trepidation, intrepid, intrepidity.

tres, three—trio, tripod, triangle, trinity, trice.

tribuo, I give—attribute, distribution, retributive.

tricæ, wiles—tricks, trickery, intricate, extricate, inextricable, intrigue, tress.

trudo (*trus*), I thrust—intrude, intrusion, extrude, protrusion.

tuber, a swelling—tubercle, tubercular, tuberose.

tueor, I observe—tutor, tuition, intuitive, tutelary.

turba, a crowd—turbulent, disturb, imperturbable, perturbation, turbid.

uber, fruitful—exuberant, exuberance.

umbra, a shade—umbrageous, umbrella, adumbrate, penumbra.

unda, a wave—undulate, undulation, redundant, inundate, abound, abundant.

ungo (*unct*), I anoint—unguent, unction, unctuous.

unus, one—uniform, unicorn, unilateral, unique.

urbs, a city—urban, urbanity, suburbs, suburban.

uro (*ust*), I burn—inure, combustion, incombustible.

utor (*us*), I use—utility, utilitarian, utensil, useful, usefulness, usury, abuse, disuse.

vaco, I am empty—vacant, vacancy, vacation, vacate.

vacuus, empty—evacuate, evacuation, vacuum.

vado, I go—evade, evasion, invade, pervade.

vagor, I wander—vagrant, vagabond, vagary, extravagance.

valeo, I am strong, I am worth—value, valor, valid, valiant, avail, valetudinarian, convalescence, invalid, prevalent.

vanus, empty—vanish, vanity, vain, vainly.

vapor, steam—vapory, evaporate, vapid, vapidness.

vario, I change—variable, various, variance, variety, variegate.

vas, a dish—vase, vascular, vessel.

vasto, I lay waste—vast, vastness, devastation, waste, wasteful.
veho, I carry—vehicle, convey, inveigh, invective.
vello (vulsi), I pull—convulsion, revulsion.
velo, I cover—veil, revelation, reveal, unveil.
velox, swift—velocity, velocimeter, velocipede.
vendo, I sell—vend, vendor, vendible, vendue, venal
ventus, the wind—vent, ventilate, ventil ation,-ator.
venio (vent), I come—convene, contravene, advent, convention, invention, revenue.
verbum, a word—verbal, verbose, adverb, proverbial.
verto (vers), I turn—verse, version, vertex, advert, aversion, adversity, perversion, universe.
verus, true—verity, veracious, verify, verdict, aver.
vestigium, a trace or mark—vestige, investigate.
vestis, a garment—vest, vestment, vestry, divest, investment.
via, a way—deviate, devious, impervious, previous, trivial, undeviating, viaduct
vicis, a change—vicar, vicarage, vicarious, vicegerent, vicissitude
video (vis), I see—vision, visible, visit, evident, providence, revise, supervision.
vigeo, I flourish—vegetable, vegetate, vegetation, vigor, vigorous, invigorate, vigil, vigilant.
villa, a farm—village, villain, villainy, villanage.
vinco (vict), I conquer—victor, convince, evince, province, vanquish, invincible
vinum, wine—vinous, vintage, vinegar, vineyard, wine.
vir, a man—virile, virility, virtue, virago, triumvirate
virus, poison—virulent, virulence.
viscus, glue—viscid, viscidity, viscous.
vita, life—vital, vitality, vitalize.
vitrum, glass—vitreous, vitrefy, vitrefaction, vitriol.
vivo, I live—vivid, vivacious, vivify, revive, convivial.
voco, I call—voice, vocal, vocation, vociferate, advocate, invocation, convoke, revoke.
volo, I am willing—voluntary, volition, benevolence, volunteer.
volo, I fly—volatile, volatility, volatilize
volvo, I roll—volume, voluble, convolve, develop, revolution, revolt.
voro, I devour—voracious, devour, carnivorous, omnivorous.
voveo, I vow—vote, votary, votive, devote, devotion.
vulgus, the common people—vulgar, ity, divulge, promulgate.
vulnus (vulner), a wound—vulnerable, vulnerary, invulnerable.

GREEK ROOTS.*

aêr, the air—aerial, aerolite, aeronaut, artery, arterial, airy, airiness.

agô, I lead—demagogue, synagogue, pedagogue, stratagem strategy.

agôn, strife—agony, antagonist, antagonism, agonize.

akouô, I hear—acoustic, acoustics, acoumeter.

angelos, a messenger—angelic, angel, archangel, evangel,-ize, ist, ism, ical.

anthrôpos, a man—anthropology, philanthropy, misanthropy.

archê, beginning, sovereignty—archaism, archives, archon, anarchy, monarchy, oligarchy, patriarch, tetrarch.

astêr, or **astron**, a star—astronomy, astronomical, astrology; aster, asterisk; astral, disaster, disastrous.

athlêtes, a wrestler—athlete, athletic.

atmos, vapor—atmosphere, atmospherical.

autos, one's self—autocrat, autograph, automaton, autonomy, autobiography, tautology.

ballô, I throw—ball, ballet, emblem, hyperbole, parable, problem, symbol, diabolical.

baptizo, I dip or sprinkle—baptist, baptism, baptismal, anabaptist, pædobaptist.

basis, the bottom—basement, baseless, abase, debase, abashed, bashful.

biblos, a book—bible, bibliography, bibliopolist, bibliomania.

bios, a life—biography, biology, amphibious.

character, a mark of distinction—character, characterize, characteristic.

charis, love, or thanks—charity, charitable, eucharist, eucharistic.

cheir, the hand—chirography, chirology, chiromancy, enchiridion, chirurgeon, (whence surgeon).

cholê, bile, anger—melancholy, choler, choleric.

christos, anointed—Christ, chrism, christen, Christianity, Christmas, antichrist.

chrôma, color—chrome, chromatics, achromatics.

chronos, time—chronic, chronicle, chronology, chronometer, anachronism, synchronous, synchronize, synchronism.

cosmos, order, the world—cosmical, cosmogony, cosmopolite, microcosm, cosmetic.

---

* The Greek letters are expressed by their English equivalent.

kranion, a skull—cranium, craniology, pericranium.
kratos, power—democratic, aristocracy, autocratic, theocracy.
krites, a judge—critic, criticism, crisis, diacritical, hypocrisy.
krupto, I hide—crypt, cryptography, apocrypha.
kuklos, a circle—cycle, encyclical, epicycle, encyclopædia, encyclopedist, cyclops.

daimon, a spirit—demon, demoniac, demonism, demonology, pandemonium.
deka, ten—decade, decalogue, decagon, hendecagon, dean.
demos, the people—demagogue, democracy, endemic, epidemic, pandemic.
despotes, a master—despotic, despotism.
dogma, *doxa*, opinion, glory—dogma, dogmatic, dogmatize, dogmatism, doxology, orthodox, heterodox, paradoxical.
dotos, given—antidote, anecdote, anecdotal.
dunamis, power—dynamics, dynameter, dynasty, dynastic.

eidos, form—asteroid, conoid, spheroid, kaleidoscope.
elektron, amber—electrical, electricity, electrify, electro-dynamics.
ergon, work—energy, liturgy, metallurgy, georgic, organ-ization.
ethnos, a nation—ethnical, ethnology, ethnographer.
ethos, custom—ethics, ethical.
eu, well (in composition)—euphony, euphemism, eulogy, eucharist, evangelist.

gamos, marriage—agamist, bigamy, misogamist, polygamy.
ge, the earth—geocentric, geography, geology, geometry, apogee, perigee.
gennao, I produce—genesis, genealogy, homogeneous, oxygen, hydrogen, nitrogen.
ginosko, I know—gnomon, gnosticism, diagnostic, physiognomy, prognostic.
glossa or *glotta*, the tongue—gloss, glossary, glossarial, glottis, epiglottis, polyglot.
gonia, an angle—pentagon, hexagon, polygon, diagonal, trigonometry.
gramma, a letter—grammar, anagram, diagram, epigram, programme, telegram.
grapho, I write—graphic, graven, autograph, epigraph, biography, geography, paragraph, telegraph, topography, &c.
gumnos, naked—gymnast, gymnastics, gymnasium.
gune, a woman—gynecocracy, misogynist, misogyny.

hedra, a seat—cathedral, sanhedrim, polyhedron, etc.
hèlios, the sun—heliocentric, helioscope, heliotrope, aphelion, perihelion, parhelion.
hémera, a day—ephemera, ephemeral, ephemeris.
heteros, another—heteroclite, heterodox, heterogeneous.
hieros, sacred—hierarchy, hieroglyphic, hierography, hierophant.
histèmi, to place—apostate, ecstacy, statics, statistic, system, systematize.
hodos, a way—episode, exodus, method,-ist,-ical, period,-ical, synod.
homos, like - homogeneous, homologous, homonymous.
hudōr, water—hydraulics, hydrogen, hydrophobia, hydrostatics, anhydrous.
humneō, I sing—hymn, hymnal, hymnology.

idios, idiom—idiot, idiocy, idiosyncrasy.
isos, equal (in composition)—isochronous, isosceles, isothermal.

lambano (*leps*), I take—syllable, catelpsy, epilepsy.
laos, the people—laity, laic, lay, as opposed to clerical.
legō, I speak or collect—lexicon, dialect, eclectic, elegy, prolegomena.
lithos, a stone—aerolite, lithography, lithotomy, monolith.
logos, a word—logic, analogy, apologue, catalogue, decalogue, dialogue, entomology, geology, neology, theology, zoology, etc.
luo, I loose—analyze, analysis, palsy, paralytic.
lyra, a lyre—lyric, lyrical, lyrist, lyrated.

machō, a fight—logomachy, monomachy, naumachy, sciomachy.
mania, madness—maniac, monomania, bibliomania.
martyr, a witness—martyr, martyrdom, martyrology, protomartyr.
manthano (*math*), learn—philomath, polymathy, mathema-tics,-tical.
mechanē, a machine—mechanic, mechanics, mechanism, machination, machinist.
melos, a song—melody, melodious, melodrama; Philomel.
mētron, a measure—metre, metrical, barometer, diameter, geometry, perimeter, symmetry, thermometer, trigonometry.
micros, small—microscopic, microcosm, micrography, micrology.
miseo, I hate—misanthropist, misogynist, misogamist.
mnēma, memory—mnemonics, mnemotechny, amnesty.
monos, one—monad, monarch, monarchy, monk, monastic, monopoly, monotheism, monotony.
morphē, shape—amorphous, metamorphose, polymorphous.
muthos, a fable—myth, mythical, mythology.

naus, a ship—nautical, nautilus, aeronaut, nausea, nauseous, nauseate.
nekros, dead—necropolis, necromancy.
nomos, a law, or rule—anomaly, antinomian, astronomy, economy.
neuron, a nerve—neuralgia, neurology, aneurism.

ode, a song—ode, epode, monody, parody, psalmody; comedy, tragedy.
oikos, a house—economy, diocese, parochial, parish.
onoma, a name—anonymous, metonymy, paronymous, patronymic, synonymous.
optomai, I see—optics, optical, optician, catoptrics, dioptrics, myopy, synopsis.
orama, a view—cosmorama, diorama, panorama.
orthos, right—orthodox, orthoepy, orthography.
osteon, a bone—osteology, periosteum.
oxus, sharp, acid—oxide, oxygen, oxytone, paroxysm.

pais, a child—pedagogue, pedagogy, pedobaptism.
pan, all (in composition)—panacea, pandemic, panoply, pantheism.
pathos, feeling—pathetic, pathology, antipathy, apathy, sympathy.
petalon, a leaf—petals, bipetalous, polypetalous, etc.
petros, a stone—petrify, petrescent, petroleum.
phago, I eat—anthropophagi, ichthyophagi, sarcophagus.
phaino, I appear—phasis, phantom, phenomenon, fantasy, sycophant.
phemi (phao), I speak—blaspheme, blasphemy, emphasis, euphemism, prophet.
phero, I bear—periphery, metaphor, phosphorus.
philos, a friend—philanthropy, philosopher, philter; Theophilus.
phone, a sound—phonetic, aphony, euphonious, symphony, cacophony.
phos, light—phosphor, phosphorus, photography, photometer.
phrasis, a phrase—phraseology, paraphrase, periphrase.
phren, the mind—phrenology, frenzy, frantic, frenetic.
phusis, nature—physic, physiology, physiognomy, metaphysics.
plasso, I form—plastic, plasm, plaster, cataplasm, protoplastic.
pneuma, the wind, a breath—pneumatics, pneumatology, pneumonic, pneumonia.
poieo, I make—poem, poet, poetical, poesy.
poleo, I sell—bibliopolist, monopoly, pharmacopolist.
polis, a city—police, policy, politic, polity, metropolis, political, cosmopolite, necropolis.
polus, many—polygon, polyglot, polysyllable.
pous (pod), a foot—antipodes, polypus, tripod.
protos, first—protomartyr, protocol, prototype, protoplast.

psallō, to play—psalm, psalmody, psalmist, psalter, psaltery.
psuchē, breath, soul—psychology, metempsychosis, psychomachy.
pur, fire—pyre, pyramid, pyrotechny, pyrometer, empyreal.

rheō, I flow—rheum, rheumatism, rhetoric, catarrh, diarrhœa, resin.

sarx, flesh—sarcasm, sarcophagy, sarcotic, anasarca.
scopeō, I see—scope, helioscope, polyscope, telescope, bishop, episcopacy, microscope, horoscope, kaleidoscope.
sophos, wise—sophism, sophistry, sophisticate, philosophy.
sphaira, a sphere—sphericity, atmosphere, hemisphere.
stereos, solid, firm—stereotype, stereoscope.
stichos, a line, a verse—distich, hemistich, decastich, acrostic.
stellō, I send—apostle, epistle.
strophē, a turning—apostrophe, catastrophe, antistrophe.

tassō, I arrange—tact, tactics, syntax.
taphos, a tomb—epitaph, cenotaph.
technē, art—technical, technology, polytechnic, pyrotechnist.
telē, afar off—telegraph, telescope, teleology, telegram.
theos, God—theism, theology, atheist, pantheon, theocracy
thermos, hot—theremometer, thermal, isothermal.
tithēmi, I place—theme, thesis, antithesis, epithet, synthesis.
tomē, a cutting—atom, atomic, anatomy, entomology, epitome, lithotomy, phlebotomy.
tonos, a sound—tone, tonic, semitone, oxytone, detonate, intonation, monotony.
tŏpos, a place—topic, topical, topography, utopian.
toxicon, poison—intoxicate, intoxication.
tropos, a turn—trope, tropical, heliotrope.
tupos, a pattern or figure—type, typical, typify, typography, anti-type, stereotype.

zōon, an animal—zodiac, zoology, zoography, zootomist; azote

www.ingramcontent.com/pod-product-compliance
Lightning Source LLC
Chambersburg PA
CBHW031445160426
43195CB00010BB/863

9783337779580